SONG OF OURSELVES

SONG OF OURSELVES

WALT WHITMAN AND THE FIGHT FOR DEMOCRACY

MARK EDMUNDSON

 Harvard University Press

Cambridge, Massachusetts & London, England   2021

Library of Congress Cataloging-in-Publication Data

Names: Edmundson, Mark, 1952– author.
Title: Song of ourselves : Walt Whitman and the fight for democracy / Mark Edmundson.
Description: Cambridge, Massachusetts : Harvard University Press, 2021. |
Includes bibliographical references and index.
Identifiers: LCCN 2020039198 | ISBN 9780674237162 (cloth)
Subjects: LCSH: Whitman, Walt, 1819–1892—Criticism and interpretation. |
Whitman, Walt, 1819–1892. Song of myself. | Democracy in literature. |
United States—History—Civil War, 1861–1865—Hospitals. | United States—
History—Civil War, 1861–1865—Literature and the war. | United States—History—
Civil War, 1861–1865—War work.
Classification: LCC PS3222.S63 E36 2021 | DDC 811/.3—dc23
LC record available at https://lccn.loc.gov/2020039198

For Liz,

beloved wife, past, present, and to come

Contents

A NOTE ON CITATIONS   ix

PREFACE   xi

Introduction   1

Part I: Song of Ourselves   13

I Celebrate Myself   15

Undisguised and Naked   19

The Marriage of Self and Soul   24

The Grass   28

All In   34

A Vision of Democracy   38

These States   44

Songs of Triumph   47

Poet of the Body   51

The Sun   53

The Generative God   61

The Animals   66

Walt Becomes Other   69

A Massacre   72

A Sea Fight   76

American Jesus   79

Democratic Götterdämmerung   84

Walt and the Priests   88

Walt's God   91

Walt and the Reader   94

Death and Democracy   99

Part II: In the Hospitals   105

Publication   107

In Washington   114

Letters Home   117

Tom Sawyer   127

The Vision Completed   133

Part III: *Song of Myself* (1855)   139

BIBLIOGRAPHY   207

ACKNOWLEDGMENTS   211

INDEX   213

A Note on Citations

All references to *Song of Myself* are to the 1855 edition, reproduced in Part III of this book, and are cited in the text by line number. The text of the poem in Part III is drawn from Walt Whitman's original 1855 *Leaves of Grass*, held by the University of Virginia Library. Citations to other works are identified by author and, where necessary, title or edition, with full references given in the Bibliography at the back of the book. "SoM" stands for *Song of Myself*, and "LoA" stands for the Library of America edition of an author's works.

Preface

This is a book about America's great poet Walt Whitman and his greatest poem, *Song of Myself*. The poem is reprinted in Part III, and I invite the reader to refer to it as the book unfolds, or to begin by taking it in from end to end. This book, like the poem it interprets, is not intended primarily for experts and scholars, but for general readers who go to literature for pleasure and instruction.

Song of Myself is a joy to read. It is magnificently eloquent and inventive, full of brilliant phrasings and rich, complex music. It affirms the pleasures of the body and wonder of the natural world. Reading it makes you feel grateful to be alive. It would have been possible to write a book about the vital aesthetic achievement of *Song* as long or longer than this one. But this book chiefly concerns another aspect of the poem.

Song of Myself is a poem about democracy. In it, Whitman offers a vision of an ideal democratic individual and democratic society. With *Song of Myself*, he attempts to inaugurate a new age, the age of authentic democracy. Democratic institutions were in place when Walt wrote, yes. But he believed that people still did not understand the true *spirit* of democracy and what it feels like at its best to live as democratic men and women every day. Democracy calls for a new literature, and in *Song of Myself* Walt tries to inaugurate it. Whitman wants democracy to be not only a form of practical governance but a form of spiritual life, the best form. Where conventional religion was, there total commitment to democracy must be, offering challenges and joys akin to those once found in transcendent faith. If democracy is only legislative and legalistic, it will fail. Democracy, Walt felt, must also be spiritual. In the transition to spiritual democracy, the poet is crucial. "The priest departs," says Walt with a pinch of irony (but not much more), and "the divine literatus comes" (Whitman, LoA, p. 932).

Some readers may feel that I idealize Walt and his *Song* in these pages. I happily admit, Walt was not always a great poet and sometimes not even a good one. And though he was a kindly and gentle man in his day-to-day life and something close to a saint in his hospital work during the Civil War, he was far from perfect. In this book, I emphasize Walt at his copious best. I want to affirm the achievements in Walt's work and in his life that can still help us to thrive as individuals and as a society. What of Whitman lives? What of Walt can we use? Unlike many literary critics, I am far less interested in who Walt *was* and how we ought to judge him than what Walt can *do* for us here and now.

Whitman is a radical writer: he was radical when he wrote, and his work is radical today. He goes further in his egalitarianism than any writer I know. Much that we currently assume about human relations is at variance with Walt's vision. He really does mean it: we are all equal; we are all one. My objective here is to lay out Whitman's vision in *Song* and to give it the most affirmative rendering that I can. I suspect that there are few readers who will embrace the vision out and out. I'm not sure that I can myself. But we need to encounter it as it is: unmitigated, subtle, and strong.

I wrote this book because I believe Whitman still has a great deal to teach us about democratic life. I don't think we've assimilated the best of his vision of what democracy means and how we might unfold it in the future. I wrote it because democracy is perpetually in danger of succumbing to the two antidemocratic forces Walt most feared. The first is hatred between Americans, the kind of hatred that Whitman saw take us to war in 1861. The second danger to democracy lies in the hunger for kings. The literature and culture that preceded Whitman and surrounded him when he wrote *Leaves of Grass* was largely what he called "feudal." It revolved around the elect, the special, the few. Walt understood human fascination with kings and aristocrats, and he sometimes tried to debunk it. But mostly he asked his readers to shift their interest away from feudalism to the beauties of democracy and the challenge of sustaining and expanding it. Democracy was in serious danger in the 1850s, when Walt began conceiving his great poem. Does one need to add that it is in danger today?

Whitman knew that democracy is ever vulnerable. It might not last. The best hope for human happiness that humankind has yet produced could disappear from the earth. Walt would not let that happen without a fight.

The text of *Song of Myself* concludes with a famous pair of lines: "Missing me one place search another, / I stop some where waiting for you" (ll. 1335–1336). But the poem doesn't really end there. Nor does it culminate in the hundreds of other poems Whitman went on to write. The true completion to *Song* occurred in the world of experience. Whitman finishes his vision not on that final page of *Song* or any other page. He completes it in the Civil War hospitals. There he went to give comfort to the sick and wounded, White and Black, Southern and Northern. In the hospitals, Whitman learns and teaches the ultimate lessons of democracy. There he becomes the sort of democratic individual that his great poem prophesies. In his life in the hospitals, Whitman is where he told us he would be. He's up ahead, waiting for us.

SONG OF OURSELVES

INTRODUCTION

Before 1855, the year Walt Whitman published the first edition of *Leaves of Grass,* he had achieved no distinction whatever. He had no formal education—no Oxford, no Cambridge; no Harvard, no Yale. His life up to his thirty-fifth year had been anything but a success. He'd been a teacher, but he was loose and a bit indolent and refused to whip his students. He'd published fiction of a dramatically undistinguished sort, and edited a Free-Soil newspaper, opposing the spread of slavery into the western territories. He'd written a good deal of journalism, but there was nothing remarkable about any of it. Much of the time, he was a working man: he was adept as a typesetter, a difficult and demanding trade, and he worked as a carpenter. In the summer of 1854, the year before the great volume appeared, he was framing two- and three-room houses in Brooklyn.

Whitman's family life was chaotic. His father, who died shortly after *Leaves of Grass* came out, had a knack for failure. Many scholars believe that the poet depicts Walter Whitman Sr. in "There Was a Child Went Forth": "The father, strong, self-sufficient, manly, mean, angered, unjust / The blow, the quick loud word, the tight bargain, the crafty lure" (LoA, p. 139). Walt's mother, Louisa Van Velsor Whitman, held the family together. She was a hardworking, capable woman who kept house well into her seventies. Walt adored her, thought of her constantly, and wrote her beautiful, affectionate letters.

Walt's brothers and sisters formed a difficult brood. Jesse, the oldest, contracted syphilis from an Irish prostitute and died in an asylum. He was prone to rage and sometimes threatened family members with a chair. Andrew Jackson was an alcoholic married to Nancy, also an alcoholic and a prostitute. Andrew and Nancy had three sons, one of whom was run over and killed while playing unwatched in Brooklyn. Edward, Walt's youngest brother, was mentally disabled and prone to fits. Eddy had a huge appetite and needed to be watched at meals because he would eat until he passed out. He lived with his mother, Louisa, until she died, then Walt took care of him. Walt's sister Hannah Louisa married an artist named Charles L. Heyde, introduced to her by Walt. Hannah and Charles moved to Vermont, where they made each other miserable. Hannah besieged the Whitman family with letters complaining about her unhappy state and provoking ongoing debates on what she ought to do.

Mary Elizabeth, the older of Walt's sisters, lived a quiet life. His brothers Thomas Jefferson and George Washington Whitman were solid and in time accomplished men. Jeff became an engineer in St. Louis; George joined the army and rose through the ranks, retiring with high honors at the end of the Civil War. As difficult as Walt's family was, he never turned away from it. He did all he could to help each and all. For their part, they loved Walt dearly, though none of them could understand a word of his poems. From this background, America's greatest poet emerged.

Whitman wrote and published the most profound and original poem that America has ever seen, the poem that in time would be called *Song of Myself. Song* has multiple dimensions; its riches are beyond count. It's a hymn to the joys of everyday human experience; it's an ode to the bounties of the natural world; it's a stirring autobiography; and much more. It's also a reflection on the nature and promise of democracy. It's an attempt to spiritualize democracy, to adapt a phrase from the writer David Brooks. In *Song,* Walt tries to give democracy the same intensity of meaning that the deepest religious faith can offer.

During lunch break in that summer of 1854, while Whitman was working as a carpenter, he liked to read. He was taken with the writings of Ralph Waldo Emerson. He surely read "Circles" and "Self-Reliance," as well as "The Poet," an essay in which Emerson called out for an authentically American bard. Sitting quietly, Whitman read that "we have yet had no genius in America, with a tyrannous eye, which knew the value of our incomparable materials" (Emerson, LoA, p. 465). I suspect that the phrase "tyrannous eye" puzzled Whitman: there was nothing especially tyrannous about him, nor would there be about his poetry. "Tyrannous eye": not quite right. But as to knowing "the value of our incomparable materials"—perhaps that was something Whitman could claim. He had seen a good deal of life. He loved to wander and look things over. He'd worked many and various jobs.

Emerson gave Whitman more. We need someone, Emerson said, who sees "in the barbarism and materialism of the times, another carnival of the same gods whose picture he so much admires in Homer" (LoA, p. 465). Barbarism and materialism, yes: Whitman would find those themes worth taking up. But the America that Whitman saw in his strolls around Manhattan and Brooklyn and during his sojourn in New Orleans was more than materialist and barbaric. America was also infused with tenderness and grace.

In "The Poet," Emerson insists on the value of American material for poetry. "Banks and tariffs, the newspaper and caucus, methodism and unitarianism, are flat and dull to dull people," he writes (LoA, p. 465). Emerson was not always well disposed to the pious and progressive literary people who surrounded him and called him their friend. He looked for a poet whose vision didn't derive chiefly from books but from life, American life as it was. One sentence in particular opens the possibility of a new world: a new poetic world but perhaps a new world for human thriving as well: "Our logrolling, our stumps and their politics, our fisheries, our Negroes, and Indians, our boasts, and our repudiations, the wrath of rogues and the pusillanimity of honest men, the northern trade, the southern planting, the Western clearing, Oregon, and Texas, are yet unsung" (LoA, p. 465).

Though America had been a nation for nearly eighty years, it was incomplete. The Declaration of Independence and the Constitution were political documents, pragmatic in their design for democracy. They were works of genius and inspired awe. Yet America lacked what Emerson called for: a vision of what being a democratic man or woman *felt* like at its best, day to day, moment to moment. America had a mind, the mind created by Thomas Jefferson and the other Founders, but we did not know our own best spirit. As Whitman puts it:

We thought our Union grand and our Constitution grand;
I do not say they are not grand and good—for they are,

I am this day just as much in love with them as you.
But I am eternally in love with you and with all my fellows upon the earth. (LoA, p. 93)

Walt's major poetry is an expression of his comradely, democratic love. Why couldn't Emerson provide the vision himself? He was a good poet and, for some time, hoped to become a great one. Many of Emerson's best-known essays have a relevant subtext. In "Self-Reliance," in "History," in "Circles," Emerson tries to open the way for imagination, his own imagination. Trust yourself, he tells his reader—and himself. Don't conform unquestioningly to established usages. Expand orbit upon orbit on the great deep. But understand that your last best effort will, in time, become a confining wall, hemming in your imagination. You must realize: men and women of real courage are never limited by their times or by the achievements of the past. Consider this: there is no history, only biography.

Nearly all of Emerson's admonitions about creativity and imagination come originally from his journals, the books he kept assiduously, volume after volume throughout his life. When Emerson tells us, in "Self-Reliance," not to be timid and apologetic but confidently strong, he is also talking to himself. Emerson affirms the struggle for originality and tries to bring originality to birth, for others and for himself. To Emerson, the supreme test of originality was poetry.

Emerson is a capable poet, but he never reached the heights he aspired to. The great poem of the United States—manifest before his eyes, though not yet on any page—he cannot create. Emerson knows what the poem of democracy should be about—"our logrolling, our stumps and their politics," "Oregon and Texas," and all the rest that remains unsung—yet the most eloquent American writer of his time, and maybe of any time, cannot find the words.

Emerson couldn't answer the call and in "The Poet" tacitly admitted as much. I can't imagine that when he asked for volunteers, he believed a jack-of-all-trades in his midthirties headed no place in particular could possibly take up the task. But that is what happened.

We had to have someone to compose the song of democracy. Emerson couldn't quite do it, implicitly admitted as much, and asked for help. Walt Whitman, uneducated, undistinguished, unproven, stepped forward. A nobody decided that he needed to redeem his nation. He'd become what he called himself in a review he wrote of his own first volume of poetry, "an American bard at last." "I was simmering, simmering, simmering," Whitman said; "Emerson brought me to a boil." The boil began in his notebooks, which he worked on during that summer of 1854 when he was framing houses. The notebook entries are often striking. In one of them, Whitman imagines himself traversing the glowing fields of heaven. During his walk, he sees Jehovah, Lord God of Hosts, Creator of Heaven and Earth and all things visible and invisible. "If I walk with Jah in Heaven," Walt says, "and he assume to be intrinsically greater than I, it offends me; and I shall certainly withdraw from Heaven" (*Notebooks*, p. 64). Walt is an American, a democratic man, and he need offer obeisance to no one, not even God.

It's possible that America's other great poet, Emily Dickinson, was also inspired by Emerson and his doctrine of self-reliance. No one was more an individual than she. Dickinson accepts no dogma, consensus, or opinion without submitting it to her brilliantly ironic imagination. She makes every intellectual and spiritual decision for herself. Though when matters are complex, she can readily live without resolution. She is perhaps the ultimate democratic individual in that she refuses to embrace any authority but her own luminous intelligence. She exemplifies the best of democracy, but she does not do what Walt does: she does not create the overarching terms for democratic life.

There was more to inspire Walt than Emerson's words. There was the opera that he loved; theater from Shakespeare to minstrel shows; the newspapers he read with relish; and his walks, interminable walks, through Manhattan, Brooklyn, and New Jersey. There were his voyages on the Brooklyn Ferry, where he seems to have experienced at least one major vision. And there were books. Whitman felt that what others regarded as the great works of literature were often admirable in their ways and that there was much to learn from them. But he also believed that they had been written to suit the needs of another world, a world in which aristocracy was ascendant. Democracy required a new literature. Its songs were yet unsung. Whitman was a product of his surroundings, as David Reynolds shows us in his fine cultural biography of the poet, but he was much, much more than that.

Many inspiring forces helped Whitman create *Song of Myself*. Yet finally, I think that it *was* Emerson who brought Whitman to his boil. He reached a hand out into the American void, and Whitman leaned close and made contact. "I speak the password primeval," Whitman says, "I give the sign of democracy" (SoM, l. 507). American democracy was going to be Whitman's subject, his inspiration, and his guide.

Whitman understood that he was a part of one of the greatest experiments since the beginning of time: the revival of democracy in the modern world. The wise believed that it probably could not succeed: the people were too ignorant, too crude, grasping, and greedy to come together and from their many create one. Who were we after all? A nation of cast-offs. We were the people who couldn't make it in the old world, a collection of crooks and failures, flawed daughters and second sons of second sons, unquestionable losers and highly dubious winners. Up to now, our betters had kept us in line: the aristocracies of Massachusetts and Virginia showed us the enlightened way and dragged us along behind. Whitman knew (and Emerson probably did too) that this could not last forever. By sheer force of numbers, or by force out and out, the outcasts and ne'er-do-wells were going to take over the nation. But under what terms?

Perhaps Emerson could not write the poem of democracy because he did not really believe that everyday people could pull together and create a plausible nation—much less the great one that Whitman foresaw. Whitman wanted us to be a beacon to the world. He wanted us to show how we the people could determine the shape of our own lives and live with joy. For make no mistake: life in a real democracy was joyful. Whitman knew this to the tips of his fingers. But how to say it, how to say it?

The Emerson who inspired Whitman while he was framing those houses in Brooklyn left him with a serious problem. No doubt Whitman thrilled to "Self-Reliance." Better perhaps than Emerson, Whitman understood that the only way to freedom was through nonconformity. Whitman was a person of strong character who treasured his individuality. There had never been anyone quite like Walt and no doubt never would be again. And Whitman, like Emerson, wished that everyone had the chance fully to become him- or herself.

But Emerson generally believed that individuals became themselves by pitting their energies against society. Society was always ready to crush the independent mind and heart. Emerson says it repeatedly. Society is a joint stock company that conspires to make the mass comfortable and ruin the truly independent woman or man. Exercise your freedom of thought, and the ignorant will cry out against you—and the learned and refined will too.

In "The American Scholar," Emerson says that the deeper the scholar dives into his private perceptions, and the more accurately he reports them to the world, the more he will find that the public delights in them. Every person will say, "this is my music; this is myself" (LoA, p. 65). In "The Poet," he conjures up the image of the one individual who speaks for all—the authentic bard.

But this is not Emerson's major key. He rarely claims that the one and the many can readily reconcile. The crowd is not his element. The people make him uneasy because they cannot think for themselves. Aside from a few wishful professions, Emerson sticks to this perception from the start of his writing life to the end.

To Emerson's vision of the conformist mass, Whitman says No. Whitman is a lover of the people, not only one at a time but collectively. He loved the experience of walking through the city, finding calm pleasure in being one of the crowd. "This is the city . . . . and I am one of the citizens," he writes, "whatever interests the rest interests me" (SoM, ll. 1070–1071). His poetry exalts the many: his catalogues of people doing their work, living their lives, and (occasionally) suffering their deaths are themselves great crowd scenes. He asks us to immerse ourselves in the teeming mass and be made whole.

But Whitman is an individualist, too. He is Walt Whitman, a kosmos, eating and drinking and breeding. In his poetry, he constantly evokes his individual beginnings and the life that he, and only he, has lived. Throughout his work, he gives voice to his particular views and visions. Whitman believes that here in America, in a true democracy, he (and the rest of us too) can have it both ways. We can enfold ourselves into the crowd of brothers and sisters and be accepted and loved. And we can speak our minds, affirm our truths, and live independent, self-reliant lives.

True democratic joy for Whitman lies in the power to be entirely your-self and yet to be accepted and affirmed by your neighbors. Is this possible? Can a society both be hospitable to difference and uphold unity? This is Whitman's gamble, and in the great poem and afterward in the hospitals, he will try to show how we can be both one and many at the same time.

I see Whitman's *Song of Myself* as an American quest. It's a coherent and continuous poem that chronicles the expansion of the poet's mind and heart. It's a poem of education and self-discovery. The objective is to travel through fields of spiritual challenge to discover and affirm a better self and a better democracy. In the poem, Walt Whitman begins as an everyday character, "one of the roughs" (l. 499). He emerges at the end as a democratic person and as an emblem for America. The poem dramatizes the struggle to engender a democratic individual, but it's also a quest to engender true democracy. Whitman doesn't only quest for himself; he quests for his nation. If he wins, we win, though we need to know how to interpret the victory.

Whitman moves in his journey from one moment of intense encounter to another. In symbolic form, he faces and by and large resolves major spiritual, political, and personal challenges. He will leave perfumes and books behind, step outside to become undisguised and naked, join self and soul in a stunning sex scene, and find the ultimate metaphor for democracy. He'll go to war with the sun, embrace sex in his own idiosyncratic way, teach us the uses of violence, become Jesus on the cross, resolve relations with God the Father, and reinterpret death. In the poem, he travels from one critical encounter to the next, taking on larger and larger challenges. His daring, imaginative encounter with Jesus, which is a climax of the poem, draws on all he has learned and achieved up until that point. In each resolved crisis encounter, Walt gains strength and then, augmented, moves on to the next and the next.

Ultimately, Whitman wants to show us how to live a righteous life that is not based on commandments and constraints. He seeks to demonstrate how our highest moral obligations can lead to happiness.

Whitman found tragic joy during the Civil War. A few years after he published the first (and to me the best) version of *Song of Myself,* Whitman moved to Washington, DC. There he did work with the wounded, sick, and dying in the military hospitals that was so unselfish, imaginatively humane, and self-sacrificing that it can still inspire awe. In the hospitals, he became a version of the large-hearted democratic individual that his poem prophesied. And there he also answered some of the questions that *Song of Myself* leaves open.

What Whitman offers now and always is hope—the hope that this new form of social life can succeed and thrive and give people access to levels of happiness and freedom that they've never enjoyed before. Whitman was not a grinning optimist. He was badly depressed when the 1855 *Leaves of Grass* failed to reach the nation. He was horribly downcast as he saw the Civil War gathering. He knew that the spiritual path he laid out in *Song* was a difficult one. Nothing the poem prophesied came as a given: it all had to be earned. What Walt offered as symbolic action remained for us to enact fully in the world, or fail to do so. Yet Walt never withdrew his hope that America could be a great nation not only for some but for all its people—and that we would be an example for others across the world.

After Emerson brought Whitman to his boil, and he produced the 1855 *Leaves of Grass,* Walt sent a copy to the Sage of Concord. Emerson wrote back what may be the most generous letter ever sent by one great writer to another. Remember: Whitman was a nobody. No one knew his name. Emerson could readily have consigned the book to the trash heap. Remember: in *Song of Myself,* Whitman achieves poetically everything that Emerson wished to achieve (and more). Remember: Emerson offered the road map, and Whitman took it. Emerson could have been overwhelmed with envy when he read *Song of Myself* and pretended not to see what was there before him.

That is not what happened. Of the 1855 *Leaves of Grass,* Emerson wrote, "I find it the most extraordinary piece of wit and wisdom that America has yet contributed. I am very happy in reading it, as great power makes us happy." It makes us happy, that is, if we can recognize it for what it asserts and what it asks of us, and not turn away. "It has the best merits," Emerson wrote, "namely, of fortifying and encouraging" (LoA, p. 1326).

So it did then. So it may now.

PART I

Song of Ourselves

I CELEBRATE MYSELF

Song of Myself genuinely begins not with words but with an image. It's an engraving of Walt Whitman, posed as what he would call "one of the roughs." He's a working man, with slouched hat and shirt open, full beard, and a look of confidence that's close to mild defiance. This man is apparently healthy (Whitman placed great stock in health), self-reliant, strong, and ready to go to work. He can take care of himself. Approach him with friendly respect, and he'll give you the same. But condescend to him—or flatter him unduly—and you'll encounter something less pleasant.

He's strong and well made. But he also has an intelligent, watchful look. He'll help you unload your wagon or pitch in to haul a barge if you ask him the right way. And unless you've arranged for pay beforehand, don't try to give him anything afterward. That would be condescending, and it would get a quick, tart reply, though probably not a rap in the jaw. The man in the engraving isn't that sort. The Whitman of *Song* likes almost everyone—though he's suspicious of teachers and preachers, and sometimes has a serious grudge (odd as it may sound) against the sun. What he most dislikes day to day, moment to moment, is any human exchange that isn't based on high-hearted equality. Friendliness—passionate democratic friendliness—means everything to Walt.

The 1855 edition of *Leaves of Grass* is not a conventionally produced book. Whitman published it himself. He designed the cover; he chose the page size; he set some of the type. The author's name appears nowhere on the cover or on the title page. We don't learn his name, "Walt Whitman, an American," until midway through the poem that will in time be called *Song of Myself,* and when we do, it marks an achievement. The poet has arrived at a new level in his quest. For as I've said, the great poem records a journey. It moves from one spiritual and conceptual achievement to the next. Walt's naming himself and designating himself an American marks a particularly significant moment in *Song*. Until the poem's midpoint, we do not know exactly who is talking to us. At the beginning, we only have the picture.

In the 1855 version of *Leaves*, the long poem that would become *Song* is nameless, as are all the poems. Over time, Whitman settled on the title by which the great poem of over a thousand lines is now known. Whitman revised the poem all through his life, until its final manifestation in the Deathbed Edition of 1892. Critics and readers differ on which version of the poem is best. (Ed Folsom and Christopher Merrill use the 1892 version for their useful book-length commentary on *Song*.) I prefer the poem's earliest iteration. It seems to me more spontaneous, fresh, and suggestive and less self-explanatory than the editions that follow it.

I think that the figure in the engraving, who has yet to earn his name, is an image of the speaker *at the beginning* of the poem. It's he who starts the poem by saying, "I celebrate myself" (SoM, l. 1). He's a depiction of the individual that Whitman calls Myself or, more illuminatingly, simply the Self. For Whitman, the Self is the being that exists in the material world. He's physical, appetitive, and earthy. He wants to live and thrive.

When Whitman starts the poem by saying, "I celebrate myself," what he means, I think, is that he celebrates the body: the physical, desire, the senses. He celebrates his being in the material world. Unlike other writers who value spirit and intellect, and deny or downgrade the body, Whitman wants to chant the praises of physical life. Emerson, in most of his work, celebrates the inner being and the creative force that abides within and is manifest in our independent thoughts and actions. Emerson begins and ends with spirit: he sometimes seems dismayed that we humans are cast in physical form, locked in a body that gets tired, grows ill, decays, and eventually dies. Whitman wants to celebrate the joys of physical life—and to transfigure its sorrows.

I think that the picture up front is the metaphorical starting point of the poem—though to be sure, Walt's preface, a prose poem in its own right, comes directly after the image. The picture embodies the condition of the poet before he undergoes the visionary journey that is *Song of Myself.* Here is Walt as a regular guy, someone who lives in the body and is determined by individual aspirations in the way most of us are. It's an imaginative achievement, and not a minor one, for Walt to comprehend who and what he is before he sets out. To begin a quest, physical or spiritual, it helps to know where you are.

Walt's identity will change through his American shamanistic journey. The Walt we are left with at the poem's close, who tells us that if we want to find him again, we'd better look under our boot soles, both is and is not the Walt on the frontispiece. He's been transformed by his vision.

"I celebrate myself," Whitman begins his great poem:

And what I assume you shall assume,
For every atom belonging to me as good belongs to you. (ll. 2–3)

Most beginning readers of Whitman think that the "you" of the second and third lines refers to the reader, and in this there's surely some truth. But the "you" that Walt is talking to—"what I assume you shall assume"— seems to me not only, and not even primarily, the reader but another part of Walt himself. Whitman is talking to his Soul. He's trying to make the Self attractive to readers, yes. But he's also attempting to present the Self in a way that will coax forward the Soul. The Soul—at least Whitman's Soul—is uneasy about entering the world as it is. Yet to Whitman, the Soul belongs in the world. It is rightly one with the physical—every atom that belongs to the Self belongs to the Soul as well, or at least it could.

In a future edition, Whitman revises the opening chant significantly. "I celebrate myself," he'll write, *"and sing myself."* The three new words connect Whitman's poem to the epic tradition. "Sing in me muse," says Homer; "I sing of arms and the man," Virgil writes. Surely *Song of Myself* isn't a full-blown epic like the *Iliad,* the *Aeneid,* or *Paradise Lost.* Whitman's poem isn't nearly as comprehensive—or lengthy. But it does share with these epics the goal of defining a culture. From Homer, the Greeks learned how to wage war, how to sacrifice, how to value martial prowess, and how to imagine the Olympian deities. Milton sought to teach the world the truths of the Christian faith as he saw them. Walt isn't systematic or encyclopedic. But Whitman does seem to hope that everything you really need to know to live as a joyful and strong citizen of the democracy is present in the poem or at least readily drawn from it by the imaginative reader. The subject of this American version of epic isn't war or religion but the expansion of spirit and consciousness, heart and mind.

"I celebrate myself / And what I assume you shall assume / For every atom belonging to me as good belongs to you." The Whitman of *Song of Myself* is melodious, eloquent. Once underway, he's prone to long, sweeping lines that sometimes possess a choral depth and sometimes seem almost to whisper: poet to reader, Walt to you. Angus Fletcher remarks that in Whitman "we recognize a persistent rhythm of anticipation, which in a traditional way may be identified with prophetic voice" (*New Literary History,* p. 308). Scholars say that *Song* is the first significant instance of *free verse.* It's unrhymed, without predictable meter and yet—Walt has a marvelous ear—as musical in its way as any poetry before or since. Free verse: free verse for a free imagination and for a free democratic individual; free verse for a free nation.

Walt begins to make his overall designs clear in the poem's next lines:

I loafe and invite my soul,
I lean and loafe at my ease . . . . observing a spear of summer grass.
    (SoM, ll. 4–5)

"I loafe and invite my soul": I think this is the Self speaking, attempting to coax the Soul forward into everyday life. But why should the Soul budge? What does Self have to offer the Soul? (And what, exactly, is this entity Walt calls Soul?) In the next seventy or so lines, Whitman does all he can to persuade the Soul to emerge and to form a full union with the Self. What would it mean to you and to me, we might ask, to merge Self and Soul? What would it mean for America to do so? Is it possible— is it even conceivable—that a country has a Self? That a nation possesses a Soul?

UNDISGUISED AND NAKED

The Soul, as we'll see, is a retiring being: mistrustful, tender, and shy. Whitman's Self will do all it can to convince the Soul to emerge from hiding. The Self is going to have to show that it's worthy of the Soul's embrace.

Walt's first move is to go outdoors. He tells us that "houses and rooms are full of perfumes" and that "the shelves are crowded with perfumes" (l. 6). He's not averse to the indoor aromas: "I breathe the fragrance myself, and know it and like it" (l. 7). It's possible that the perfumes on the shelves are a metaphor, a metaphor for books and official culture, what's already been said and thought. Whitman's not resentful about indoor culture or the riches of civilization. He begins the introduction to *Leaves* declaring that "America does not repel the past or what it has produced" (LoA, p. 5). We don't repel the past per se: we simply turn from it and start again. Whitman admits that official culture can "intoxicate" (l. 8), but he's determined not to let it.

Whitman believes that his poetry will begin a new epoch. Most writing up until 1855 had been *feudal:* that is, it celebrated the aristocratic, the rich, the extraordinary. Whitman devotes himself to writing about the common and everyday: that's the kind of poetry a democracy needs. We're done with kings, done with potentates of all sorts. Yet Whitman doesn't rage against the aristocratic past. His temperament is gentle. He wants to pass beyond the old royal ways without rebellious anger, though he's quite certain that we must give those ways up, and forever.

The past—indoor life and cultural intoxicants—aren't what Whitman needs if he's going to *invite* his Soul into the world and have it accept the invitation. He wants the pure outdoor atmosphere. And he wants a new beginning. "I will go to the bank by the wood and become undisguised and naked" (l. 11), Walt says.

He's got to get outside and bathe in the "odorless" atmosphere, the fresh and uncompromised natural air. He needs to get his clothes off, as though he's just being born or reborn. He's an American Adam—a useful term put forward by the critic R. W. B. Lewis—who wants to begin life all over. Democracy is new in the modern world: it's got to be celebrated in fresh terms with a new kind of poem.

Whitman is "naked," not "nude." The nude is stylized, aesthetic: it's an individual posed for a painting or a sculpture. Nudity is an indoors, protected state sanctioned by culture. Being naked is something else. Nakedness is about being vulnerable and open to fresh experience. The nude looks down on the naked from a cultured height. Whitman is of the party of nakedness. The kids who took off their clothes and slid in the mud at Woodstock were naked, not nude. To be naked is to align yourself with nature against excessive refinement and cultivation. By all rights, nudist colonies should call themselves nakedness colonies.

Being naked means shedding as much needless socialization as you can and getting rid of as many preconceptions as possible. Check your beliefs indoors and get out into nature. "You must become an ignorant man again," says Wallace Stevens to his ephebe, or beginning poet, "and see the sun with an ignorant eye" (p. 207). Whitman is trying to achieve a certain sort of ignorance by shedding his clothes and going out to the bank. Thus Thoreau: "How can he remember well his ignorance—which his growth requires—who has so often to use his knowledge" (p. 4). To be naked is also to jettison identifying class markers. Clothes tell the world who we are and where we fit in the social scheme. Whitman doesn't care for social hierarchies, and he shows as much by tossing his clothes aside.

By shedding his clothes, Walt, in his incarnation as the Self, has become nearly as vulnerable as the recessive Soul will prove to be. But apparently that's not enough for the Soul to accept his invitation and emerge. The Soul requires more blandishments, more possibilities.

What does the Self have to offer the Soul that can get it to accept the invitation and come out from hiding? Why shouldn't the Soul stay where it is, wound into the recesses of Walt's being?

Walt offers the Soul the pleasures of embodied life. Come out, he says. Come out—there are wonders here: the wonders of the body, first. Come out and possess them: they're yours by right. Whitman offers

> My respiration and inspiration . . . . the beating of my heart . . . . the passing of blood and air through my lungs,
> The sniff of green leaves and dry leaves, and of the shore and darkcolored sea-rocks, and of hay in the barn,
> The sound of the belched words of my voice . . . . words loosed to the eddies of the wind,
> A few light kisses . . . . a few embraces . . . . a reaching around of arms,
> The play of shine and shade on the trees as the supple boughs wag,
> The delight alone or in the rush of the streets, or along the fields and hillsides,
> The feeling of health . . . . the full-noon trill . . . . the song of me rising from bed and meeting the sun. (ll. 15–21)

See what bounties I have for you, Whitman's Self tells his Soul (and Walt tells his reader), the bounties of ecstatic physical life, good humor, and good health. Smell, sound, sight: these are the joys of being embodied, and you, my Soul, can share them. Then there's the joy of touch, the erotic joy, slipped in for the delectation of the Soul. What if sex could be physical and *spiritual* too? What if embraces and kisses were more than a matter of Self: desire, the appetites?

Even before Whitman is a political poet, a poet of democracy, he is a poet of joy. First-time readers are exhilarated by his uncanny power to evoke the bliss in being alive. Reading Whitman, one feels grateful simply to be. Worries pass away, fears diminish, the past and future fade, and one lives, along with Walt, in the gorgeous moment. Maybe this magnificent immediacy becomes more available in a democracy, where one can stop looking up, at those who are purportedly superior to you, and down, at those who seem to be less. When you leave hierarchy and hierarchical thinking, Walt suggests, you are free from false confinements and can live joyously in the present. You don't need to look up or down, but can gaze *out* into the world.

Day and night Whitman is surrounded by the world of the Self and other Selves. The horizons of this life seem to be composed by "the latest news .... discoveries, inventions, societies .... authors old and new, / My dinner, dress, associates, looks, business, compliments, dues, / The real or fancied indifference of some man or woman I love" (ll. 60–62). Whitman doesn't mind being immersed in the everyday world, not at all. But he tells us, and tells his Soul, that there's more to life than that. The Soul stands calm and apart, awaiting its proper moment. Says Walt of everyday life and events, "They come to me days and nights and go from me again, / But they are not the Me myself" (ll. 64–65). Walt lets the Soul, or Me Myself, know that he's aware of its being, he honors it, and that he'll try to bring it out into the world of experience.

Whitman has made the way safe and enticing for his vulnerable, delicate Soul to emerge, and so it does:

Apart from the pulling and hauling stands what I am,
Stands amused, complacent, compassionating, idle, unitary,
Looks down, is erect, bends an arm on an impalpable certain rest,
Looks with sidecurved head curious what will come next,
Both in and out of the game, and watching and wondering at it.
    (ll. 66–70)

The spirt that Whitman coaxes forth is tender, observant, and vulnerable. It's neither male nor female, exhibits no race or class. It's gentle and kindly ("compassionating") and sweetly curious, wanting to see what will come next, but not desperate to know. It's able to look at the world—"both in and out of the game"—without judgment. It seems to take great pleasure in observing all that passes. Walt's Soul is whole and complete in itself—"unitary." One feels an intense sweetness and tenderness, and one worries that this Me Myself, or Soul, might at any moment withdraw to a place of greater safety.

Whitman's Soul is a figure of watchful sensitivity, what Harold Bloom would call "the poet within the poet." It is surely too vulnerable to step undefended into the world as it is. Walt, one of the roughs, offers the Soul joy—the joy of physical life—but the Self also seems to offer the Soul protection. Whitman feels confident enough to expose the most tender part of himself under the protection of the most worldly.

How idiosyncratically *poetic* this mapping of the interior life, Self and Soul, might initially seem. Actually it's quite pragmatic. Suppose we were to say of this or that individual that his Self and his Soul don't know each other at all. Or, his Self and his Soul were once together and in harmony—but now they're separated. To the reader of Whitman, this would make complete sense. One would be saying that what is most tender and sensitive and what is toughest and most worldly in this individual have fallen away from each other when they actually need each other to thrive. He can be tough—but he quickly becomes harsh and even cruel. (He's all Self.) He can be sweet, but quickly become treacly, weak. (He's Soul and nothing but.) "Lacks one lacks both" (l. 45), as Whitman wisely says.

By bringing the Soul forward into day-to-day life, Whitman has crossed a threshold. He's taken a step forward in his quest.

THE MARRIAGE OF SELF AND SOUL

It's not enough for Whitman to coax the Soul forward: Self and Soul must marry for Whitman to continue his quest to create a vision of spiritual democracy. There are a number of shocking moments in the poem: the first of them occurs after the Self has beckoned the Soul forward. "I believe in you my soul" (l. 73), he says. In other words: Stay steady, don't draw back—I can protect you. "I believe in you my soul . . . . the other I am must not abase itself to you / And you must not be abased to the other" (ll. 73–74). Soul must not dominate Self; Self must not dominate Soul. Walt demands perfect equality in the social world but also in the interior world.

There follows then what can only be described as a love scene between Self and Soul:

> Loafe with me on the grass . . . . loose the stop from your throat,
> Not words, not music or rhyme I want . . . . not custom or lecture,
>   not even the best,
> Only the lull I like, the hum of your valved voice.
>
> I mind how we lay in June, such a transparent summer morning;
> You settled your head athwart my hips and gently turned over
>   upon me,
> And parted the shirt from my bosom-bone, and plunged your
>   tongue to my barestript heart,
> And reach till you felt my beard, and reached till you held my feet.
>   (ll. 75–81)

This, as I understand it, is the Self describing an erotic encounter in which the once shy Soul becomes aggressive: you "plunged your tongue to my barestript heart." It's now the Self that is vulnerable: its heart has become naked and fully present.

What's going on here? I don't think it's too much to say that Walt's Soul is ravishing Walt's Self. The Soul has become actively desiring. It lies down with the Self and settles its head athwart the Self's hips and reaches it arms out from beard to feet—a long-armed Soul, this one. The head athwart the hips? Is this fellatio? The eventual target of the Soul's tongue is Whitman's heart. That indicates that the Soul has penetrated the Self far enough so that the Self is no longer wary of the tenderness that the Soul embodies. The Self's heart is more now than just a physical organ: it's a center of compassion, feeling. Readers have spoken of Whitman's extraordinary "delicacy." Precisely so. Whitman achieves his delicacy by opening himself to the Soul.

The two parts of his being have become one, imaginatively at least. The Self is not abasing itself to the Soul; the Soul isn't abased to the Self. To Whitman, abasement is the worst possible act. It smacks of aristocracy and Whitman's major cultural foe, feudalism. Self and Soul are married as equals in this strange ceremony. At last, Self and Soul are one.

Whitman's soul is far different from the Christian Soul, which is often understood as a spiritual ledger that chronicles the individual's ratio of sin to grace. It's the book that Saint Peter and the Lord will read on the day of passage into the next life when the Soul earns salvation or goes to eternal fire. Whitman de-divinizes the Soul, just so (as we'll see) he de-divinizes the spiritual life overall. Though Whitman's Soul is sacred, it exists without reference to God or Satan.

The Soul is proud, Whitman often tells us—"the soul has measureless pride" (p. 13), Walt says in the preface to the poem. It refuses to be dominated, refuses to be abased to anyone or anything. "Pride" is a critical word in Whitman, and he uses it in his own way. Walt associates "pride" with democratic dignity, not with aristocratic entitlement. Pride isn't the sin of Satan. It's the sign of American self-respect and respect for others. The proud individual will not be dominated. She will not signify her obeisance even to God. And she will not dominate others.

The Soul has another dimension as well. As Walt says in the preface, "The soul has that measureless pride which consists in never acknowledging any lessons but its own. But it has sympathy as measureless as its pride and the one balances the other and neither can stretch too far while it stretches in company with the other" (p. 13). The compassionate Soul takes one into the hearts of others. And it surely also mitigates any aspiration to dominance that the Soul's pride might be holding in abeyance. But the Soul also protects the individual against the domination of others.

In a hierarchical world, the Soul might choose to stay in hiding to avoid humiliations. But in a world without superiors and inferiors, the Soul's humane, democratic pride can stay intact. More readily, then, the Soul—that which is most gentle and perceptive in the individual—can move abroad in the world. People may become more sympathetic, and also more creative, in a culture where they can sustain their dignity all the time. They will not have to surround themselves with defenses to fend off insults, implicit and overt, from others. Nor will they have to defend against expressing their more tender impulses, for fear that doing so will make them vulnerable. Democracy, Whitman suggests, is where the Soul can be most free. It's where culture can be most creative and humane.

If an individual can conjoin Self and Soul, is it possible that a nation, a democratic nation, can do so? Perhaps Whitman wants to offer us a vision not just of the well-balanced democratic individual but of the democracy proper. What would it mean for a nation's Self to marry its Soul?

Can nations be said to have Selves? Said to have Souls? Is it possible for the polis to mirror the psyche? Plato, a great enemy of democracy, thought so. In his vision of the soul, as in his vision of the political realm, reason must rule. The philosopher kings stand above the people, both the warriors and the craftspeople; so the rational faculties abide above the appetitive and the spirited parts of the soul. For Whitman, matters are different: his image of being, political and personal, is not hierarchical like Plato's but dialectical. Self and Soul need to be in harmony. We require defense, protection, and security. But we also need humane sensitivity and imagination.

Sometimes it seems that the nation, like a certain sort of individual, is not dialectical, mobile, and practical but split and stubborn. We don't know how to be both strong and compassionate; we can't understand how to merge the two sides of Whitman's dialectic and keep them moving. The more refined lack all sense of power and force; and the worldly cannot see kindness and care for the virtues they are. Each side confronts the other by consolidating its stubbornly inert persona and seeks to win out not through dialogue but through suppression and domination. Rage replaces humane exchange. We need to be reminded, and Whitman does remind us, that we in this democracy are brothers and sisters—all of us, from the most to the least. We may grow angry with each other. But we must never despise each other or hold each other in contempt. We cannot look down, or stare up in awe, at brothers and sisters. We must be—and here is a word that Whitman loved and Lincoln, who came to mean so much to Walt, did too—in a democracy, we must strive to be Friends.

THE GRASS

Whitman's readers often ask where, exactly, his amazing poetry came from. How did he generate his eloquence and invention? Up until 1855, Whitman wrote nothing of real distinction. There were dozens of journalists as good or better. He showed no genuine originality, no capacity for a major vision. How was his great poetry born?

As you read through Whitman's early journal entries, you quickly perceive Walt's delight in discovering his Soul. His initial thoughts about it are abrupt and uncertain, but there's a sense of exhilaration there too at finding a part of himself he hadn't really known before. "The soul or spirit transmutes itself into all matter" (*Notebooks,* p. 57). "I guess the soul itself can never be any _____? Thing but great and pure and immortal; but it makes itself visible only through matter" (p. 58). Perhaps most important, "Every soul has its own individual language, often unspoken, or lamely feebly haltingly spoken but a true fit for that man and perfectly adapted to his use" (pp. 60–61). Walt saw that there was some part of him that spoke haltingly or maybe didn't speak at all. But it had great promise. Once he gave a name to this submerged part, appropriating the religious term to his own uses, he could begin to tap into its powers.

Walt saw that he was more than a Self. He was also a Soul. And if he gave that Soul voice, in conjunction with the Self, who knows what he might achieve? Up until then, he had been writing with only half of his resources, representing only a part of his being. Now he could allow his tenderness and compassion into his work, and not just write as his worldly Self. Perhaps most of us write and think and even live from only a part of ourselves. Who knows what is within, unnamed and as yet untapped?

By merging Self and Soul, worldliness and sensitivity, Whitman reaps benefits. His vision enlarges: he can see more, know more. Whitman's imagination now becomes mobile and expansive. Through the merger of Self and Soul, fresh perceptions come. "Swiftly arose and spread around me the peace and joy and knowledge that pass all the art and argument of the earth" (SoM, l. 82). He knows that all men are his brothers and all women his sisters and lovers; he feels at one with God, and he sees the wonder of the creation, down to the "mossy scabs of the wormfence, and heaped stones, and elder and mullen and pokeweed" (l. 89). (Wormfence? It's a zigzag fence made of interlocking rails, held up by cross poles.) Walt sees high and low, and finds both strange and wonderful.

Whitman understands that everything that exists is a miracle, the "brown ants in the little wells" (l. 88) as much as God himself. Democratic vision perceives the sacredness of all that is. This knowledge becomes Walt's on an intimate level when he dares to expose his tenderest and most imaginative part, under the protection of his worldly side. When he gets the ratio of defense and sensitivity right, sealing the conjunction with erotic intensity, he's rewarded with an enhanced sense of being and with visionary powers.

Alive with fresh capacities, Whitman achieves his central image for democracy, the grass: "A child said, What is the grass? fetching it to me with full hands" (l. 90).

Whitman says that he does not know what the grass *is* any more than the child does. He cannot—and won't—offer a literal answer to the question. Instead Whitman spins into a litany of "guesses." The grass is the flag of Whitman's disposition, "out of hopeful green stuff woven" (l. 92); it's "the handkerchief of the Lord" (l. 93); it "is itself a child . . . . the produced babe of the vegetation" (l. 96); it's "the beautiful uncut hair of graves" (l. 101). The grass reminds Whitman of the beards of old men and the faint red roofs of the mouths of the dead. He offers one metaphor for the grass after another—and one feels that now, in his new incarnation, he could go on forever. Walt's power of metaphor making has become fully activated by what he's achieved with the merger of Self and Soul. Aristotle says that metaphor making is an indelible sign of genius and cannot be learned from others. And indeed Whitman has acquired it for and by himself.

The grass is many things, but chiefly, the grass is the sign of equality, equality within democratic America:

Or I guess it is a uniform hieroglyphic,
And it means, Sprouting alike in broad zones and narrow zones,
Growing among black folks as among white,
Kanuck, Tuckahoe, Congressman, Cuff, I give them the same, I
    receive them the same. (ll. 97–100)

We are all—Black and White and Red, everyday people and distinguished statespersons—blades of grass, nothing more or less. We arise from nature, and to nature, the grass, we return. But here is Whitman's crucial paradox: by affirming ourselves as nothing but leaves of grass, we become more than individual leaves. We become part of the beautiful unity—out of many, one—that is the field of green blades shining beneath the sky.

Whitman has found a magnificent metaphor for democratic America and its people. We are like the grass. No two grass blades are alike: they're a little like snowflakes. Each one has its own being. Each has a certain kind of chlorophyll-based individuality. Yet step back and you'll see: the blades are all more like each other than not. And what are these blades of grass but an emblem for Americans? We are different from each other, but we are also at least as much alike as we are different, and probably more so. This place, this America, is where we can be ourselves to the utmost and yet share deep kinship with our neighbors. And who are our neighbors? Kanuck, Congressman, Tuckahoe, Cuff—Canadian, legislator, Virginia planter, Black man, all of the teeming blades of grass that we see around us.

Together, the blades of grass create an expanse of green—a verdant quilt that covers the ground. When you stand back far enough, you can't see any of the individual blades. They form a whole—an organic unity. But look closer and there they are, the grass blades, vibrant and unique—no two alike. We say: e pluribus unum. We say: from many one. But who could have envisioned what that would look like and how it would feel before Whitman came along?

From the grass, if one listens and looks with an open heart, one can begin to draw secrets. The grass speaks to Whitman. And it begins to offer hints about the greatest of all human mysteries, the mystery of death. Whitman says that the blades of grass are "so many uttering tongues" (l. 110):

> I wish I could translate the hints about the dead young men and
>   women,
> And the hints about old men and mothers, and the offspring taken
>   soon out of their laps. (ll. 112–113)

Then, with his enhanced powers, Whitman sees that he can *begin* to translate those hints. Where are the dead? "They are alive and well somewhere" (l. 116). And then what may be among the most important lines of the poem: "The smallest sprout shows there is really no death, / And if ever there was it led forward life, and does not wait at the end to arrest it" (ll. 117–118). How could this be? It surely sounds anything but logical. A sprout shows there is no death? It will take us until the end of the poem to understand this line and Walt's vision of death and democracy. But on what may be the poem's most important issue—the issue of death—Walt has made a beginning.

Walter offers the grass passage to the reader as a thought experiment. Try imagining yourself as a blade of grass, one blade among a beautiful profusion. You're not identical to the blades around you, but you're not far from being so. At any moment you might emphasize your singularity—what makes you unusual among the mass. Or you might emphasize your identity with the blades that surround you—your solidarity with all. Sometimes you may not feel that you are much of anything in yourself, but the effect that you help create overall—the green world of democracy—is formidable. You have the comfort of unity; and you have the pride and focus that comes from individuality. We are all so many "uttering tongues."

The grass is Whitman's answer to the problem that bedeviled Emerson: how to resolve the tension between the individual and the group. Recall that Emerson is sometimes hopeful. When you speak your deep and true thoughts, no matter how controversial, in time the mass of men and women will come around to you. Each will say, "this is my music, this is myself" (Emerson, LoA, p. 65). But mostly Emerson is skeptical about getting the one and the many to cohere. Society is almost inevitably the enemy of genius, or even individuality. Whitman's trope of the grass suggests that the one and the many can merge. But I'm not sure that Emerson would find the distinction between one grass blade and another to be enough to account for the distinction between the individual of genius and the ordinary, rather unenlightened soul. To Whitman, the poetic genius, the president of the United States, and the everyday working man really are close enough to be compared to one blade of grass and another. But this is something that Whitman will need to prove, both in his poem and beyond it in the world of experience.

With the discovery of the democratic metaphor of the grass, Whitman has crossed another threshold on his quest. He now understands *and feels* how equal we are, person to person, being to being. And that discovery allows him to make loving, admiring connection with all the people around him. Whitman's discovery of the grass lets him imagine a world without significant hierarchy. (Can any distinct blade of grass be all that much more important than any other?) In it, we are equal, part of one great human and material body.

When you embrace the metaphor of the grass—make the grass the national flag, as it were—you get to love and appreciate all the people who surround you. You become part of a community of equals. You can feel at home. Knowing what he knows, feeling what he feels, Whitman can now take us on a tour of the democracy and show us what we might achieve by following him. What he is dramatizing in the famous catalogues of people doing what they do every day is quite simple. These are your brothers, he effectively says. These are your sisters. Figuratively speaking, the marriage of Self and Soul gave Walt the imaginative power to create the metaphor of the grass. So the grass metaphor leads Walt on to more invention, to his amazing catalogues.

Affection and friendship can rule the day. There is no reason to sweat and strain and compete and seek the highest point. You are at peace here. You are home. Relax (or "loafe," one of Whitman's favorite words and acts, or anti-acts) and enjoy the experience of being. This is a party that everyone is invited to. In general, we walk the streets with a sense of isolation. We're individuals, monads. But if we can move away from our addictions to hierarchy and exclusive individuality, and embrace Whitman's trope of the grass, our experience of day-to-day life can be different. We can look at those we pass and say not, "That is another." Instead we can say, "That too is me. That too I am." Or so Whitman hopes.

Of course, an effort is involved. Whitman's benefits do not come for free, or simply by reading his poem. We've got to meet his vision halfway: by being amiable, friendly, humane, and nonhierarchical. As we'll see, this repudiation of hierarchy is not so easy. It's not clear that even Whitman himself pulls it off. (Isn't he trying to be a *great poet* here? The first truly American bard?) The inscription to the final edition of *Leaves* begins, "One's self I sing, a simple separate person / Yet utter the word democracy, the word En-Masse" (LoA, p. 165). Is it possible to be a simple separate person and yet fully part of the mass?

ALL IN

Who counts in the democracy? Who's part of the expanding vision? Whitman's answer to that question is obvious: everyone is, or should be. After his discovery of the sacred emblem of the grass, Whitman moves out, a bit uncertainly at first, to begin welcoming in as many people as possible.

Whitman's present at harvest time: "I am there .... I help .... I came stretched atop of the load" (SoM, l. 164). He's a crewman on a Yankee clipper: "I bend at her prow or shout joyously from the deck" (l. 174). He's a hunter in the western territories, choosing a safe spot to pass the night, kindling a fire and broiling fresh-killed game. He's off digging clams with the boatmen: "I tucked my trowser-ends in my boots and went and had a good time, / You should have been with us that day round the chowder-kettle" (ll. 176–177). Democracy is about enjoying your life in the world. You can join in and take your pleasures with most any group, because you're not above them and not below. You're always welcome and welcoming. It's right to join the harvest, right to hop on the clipper, right to go with the hunter, fine to dig clams in company. Says Whitman, "[I] went and had a good time" (l. 176). What else should democracy be about but having a good time with friends? And potential friends—equals, comrades—are everywhere.

Whitman pushes further. He's there, he says, at the marriage of the frontiersman and his Indian bride. "I saw the marriage of the trapper in the open air in the far-west .... the bride was a red girl" (l. 178). It's a blending of the races—an enlargement of the democratic community by one of the most expeditious ways we know, intermarriage. Marrying across racial and religious lines was and is one of the best ways to help people merge with each other in the democratic community. Many of us know that now. Whitman knew it in 1855.

"The runaway slave came to my house" (l. 183), says Whitman. As far as we know, none ever did in his day-to-day life. The everyday Whitman of 1855 was not an abolitionist out and out. He wrote against the spread of slavery into the western territories, but he was not ready to go to war to rid the nation of it. His politics were much like Lincoln's: preserve union first; the Union above all. Yet here he is, in imagination at least, seeming to flout the Fugitive Slave Law, which dictated that slaves who escaped into the free states had to be returned to their masters. "He staid with me for a week before he was recuperated and passed north, / I had him sit next me at table . . . . my firelock leaned in the corner." (ll. 191–192). The firelock is there, presumably, to fight off slave catchers, should they burst in. Whitman's hospitality may seem slightly patronizing, but his defiance, in imagination, of unjust law rings out.

Walt depicts a muscular Black man plowing and tells us that he loves this giant (l. 224). And he becomes a slave on the run, hounded by dogs (ll. 834–839). Some people now think that a White man cannot render the experience of a Black one—it is forbidden, unjust. But Walt does so, and I think he will outlast all of his detractors.

> I am the hounded slave . . . . I wince at the bite of the dogs,
> Hell and despair are upon me . . . . crack and again crack the
>   marksmen,
> I clutch the rails of the fence . . . . my gore dribs thinned with the
>   ooze of my skin,
> I fall on the weeds and stones,
> The riders spur their unwilling horses and haul close,
> They taunt my dizzy ears . . . . they beat me violently over the head
>   with their whip-stocks. (ll. 834–839)

Most slaves could not read or write. Should no one bear imaginative witness for them?

True democracy is about cultivating the ability to enter the minds and hearts of all of our fellow citizens, or at least trying to. We'll no doubt do it imperfectly—and perhaps at times Walt does. But empathy is a condition that we need to cultivate. Whitman can help. When people censure writers for attempting to connect across the borders of class and race and gender, they are inhibiting the expansion of democracy. Does a certain identification smack of cliché? Is it too easy, reductive? Point it out—and then with charity and a high heart, ask for better. I find Walt's connections with others persuasive—though not always perfect. Overall, in his powers of identification and empathy, I think he is still out ahead of us.

Of women and women's rights, women's sexuality, Walt is a free-wheeling prophet. He describes twenty-eight young men bathing close to the shore, laughing and playing in the spume. Looking down from her mansion is a twenty-eight-year-old woman, confined by probity, confined by stale mores. Down she comes, in her imagination (and Walt's), frol-icking with the bunch of them. "Which of the young men does she like the best? / Ah the homeliest of them is beautiful to her" (ll. 198–199). Sud-denly she's there and taking all the joy in her body and spirit that the young men do:

> Dancing and laughing along the beach came the twenty-ninth
> bather,
> The rest did not see her, but she saw them and loved them.
>
> The beards of the young men glistened with wet, it ran from their
> long hair,
> Little streams passed all over their bodies.
>
> An unseen hand also passed over their bodies,
> It descended tremblingly from their temples and ribs.
>
> The young men float on their backs, their white bodies swell to the
> sun . . . . they do not ask who seizes fast to them,
> They do not know who puffs and declines with pendant and bending
> arch,
> They do not think whom they souse with spray. (ll. 202–210)

Come on. Join in. The invitation arrives through some marvelous word-painting. You can see, hear, feel the scene. ("The beards of the young men glistened with wet, it ran from their long hair, / Little streams passed all over their bodies" [ll. 204–205].) The young woman joins now in imagination, Whitman's and her own as Whitman conceives it. In time maybe she can do so in life.

She's escaping more than stiff morality: she's escaping her money, her so-called privilege. Is it possible to have a *good time* in the democracy if you're rich? Possible, surely it's possible. But it's far less likely than if you're not. Whitman never cries out for socialism or major economic reorganization. (Though he does once point to "Many sweating and plowing and thrashing, and then the chaff for payment receiving, / A few idly owning, and they the wheat continually claiming" [ll. 1068–1069].) But he indicates all the time that money and status are impediments to joining in the thriving life of this new America. Give them up and see what happens.

Richard Rorty describes the progress of democracy as the expansion of the number and type of people who can come together under the rubric of "we." That's what Whitman's up to here, expansion. The tent grows larger, the family increases: famers, sailors, hunters, clam diggers, runaway slaves, women imprisoned by their wealth and narrow virtue. No one need stand at the door. No one is left out.

You join the democratic community, become a blade of grass, because it leads you to a more joyous existence than you could otherwise have. Aristocracy—and there are many forms of aristocracy—cuts you off from the kinds of connection with others that make life worth living. There's no real joy in feudalism. But democracy as Whitman conceives it is not so easy to achieve.

A VISION OF DEMOCRACY

After the epiphany of the grass, Whitman's sense of being is enlarged. His poetic power expands:

> What is commonest and cheapest and nearest and easiest is Me,
> Me going in for my chances, spending for vast returns,
> Adorning myself to bestow myself on the first that will take me,
> Not asking the sky to come down to my goodwill,
> Scattering it freely forever. (ll. 252–256)

And then Whitman's first grand democratic flight begins:

> The pure contralto sings in the organloft,
> The carpenter dresses his plank . . . . the tongue of his foreplane whistles its wild ascending lisp,
> The married and unmarried children ride home to their thanksgiving dinner,
> The pilot seizes the king-pin, he heaves down with a strong arm,
> The mate stands braced in the whaleboat, lance and harpoon are ready,
> The duck-shooter walks by silent and cautious stretches,
> The deacons are ordained with crossed hands at the altar,
> The spinning-girl retreats and advances to the hum of the big wheel,
> The farmer stops by the bars of a Sunday and looks at the oats and rye,
> The lunatic is carried at last to the asylum a confirmed case,

He will never sleep any more as he did in the cot in his mother's
    bedroom,
The jour printer with gray head and gaunt jaws works at his case,
He turns his quid of tobacco, his eyes get blurred with the
    manuscript;
The malformed limbs are tied to the anatomist's table,
What is removed drops horribly in a pail;
The quadroon girl is sold at the stand . . . . the drunkard nods by the
    barroom stove,
The machinist rolls up his sleeves . . . . the policeman travels his
    beat. (ll. 257–273)

Whitman is moving through space at visionary speed, seeing what there
is to see of American life: focusing on this and that striking individual
(this or that striking blade of grass) and also creating an expansive image
of the whole (the field of grass—"the flag of my disposition, out of hopeful
green stuff woven" [l. 92]) that is America. The singularity of each being
matters, and their collective identity does too. You become more an individual by being a part of this group; the group becomes richer for con-
taining so many different living, breathing types. The "confirmed case"
is part of the great unity, as much as the serene deacons being confirmed
in holy orders. One senses that virtually every scene Whitman depicts
could expand into a full narrative: the lunatic and the jour (journal)
printer get two lines apiece and could no doubt get more, as all the others
surely could.

I said that Whitman thought of his poem as at least in some measure
an American epic. ("I sing myself," he adds in that epic-evoking revision
to his opening.) In the *Iliad*, Homer offers the catalogue of the Greek
ships, organized by the importance of the warriors they carried, with em-
phasis on the chieftains. In *Paradise Lost*, Milton gives us a catalogue of
the major demons cast into hell. Whitman has his catalogue too. It's not
composed of the greatest or fiercest or most formidable but of everyday
American men and women, all equal, all one. His catalogues suggest that
Homer's and Milton's are antiquated, aspects of vanished, or vanishing,
cultures.

Whitman creates imaginative community with his poetic catalogues.
When we are at work, we are often isolated, or confined to a small group,

even in a flourishing democracy. We can't see all of our fellow Americans working away at their tasks: can't see the farmer, the deacons, the spinning girl. But Whitman brings them to us in his catalogues. He makes them manifest in our imaginations as we go about our own daily labors. By doing so, he helps us feel part of a group, part of a larger whole. Work can be isolating and lonely. But when you can imagine all the many others who are laboring to create human well-being, you can feel part of a rich community.

Reading a Whitman catalogue can be exhilarating. It feels good to be part of the growing, thriving community that he depicts. It can fill a reader with joy. *Song* is more than merely a political statement. The poem also allows you to experience the emotion that infuses day-to-day democratic life at its best.

What about that quadroon girl in Whitman's catalogue? What do we make of the fact that she's in bondage and probably on her way to a life of servitude and violation? It's not an easy question. I think that by putting her in his list, Whitman makes her equal to all the others he names. And if that is so, shouldn't she be as free as any of them at their best of times? All human beings deserve respect and compassion. As Whitman will say later in the poem, "By God! I will accept nothing which all cannot have their counterpart of on the same terms" (l. 508). A little vague, but one gets the idea. When Whitman arrives at the end of this, his first grand catalogue, he says, "And such as it is to be of these more or less I am" (l. 325).

Whitman's vision can sound appealing. Who wouldn't want to be part of everyone and everything? Who wouldn't want to feel the presence of all of one's fellows in the democracy, not in Darwinian, competitive ways but calmly, affectionately? Who wouldn't want to be a true egalitarian? But matters are more complicated. Nothing is got for nothing, and it helps to know what Whitman asks us to affirm and what he asks us to deny, or even repudiate, to be his fellow democrats. What would it mean, we might ask, to reject the image of the grass and the flight of egalitarian imagination it makes possible—what would it mean to reject democracy as Whitman so far envisions it?

One might react against the naturalism of the image. The grass is merely physical—it doesn't connect itself in any way to the creator, to theology, to heaven and hell. You might say No to any commanding conception of life that doesn't make God central. (Whitman has a good deal to say about God and religion later in the poem, but ultimately he does not worship God—he worships the democracy.) So you might miss the theological dimension of life—spiritualized democracy might not be enough for you.

Then too you might resist the collective tendency of the image. You don't want to be one among many; you want to distinguish yourself above the rest and be a single and singular being that all look to with admiration. You want there to be more difference between you and your neighbor than the differences between one blade of grass there in the meadow and the next. I'm guessing that this is what Emerson would have felt, for he believed that society advances through the contribution of the great. For Walt, democracy offers a certain kind of pleasure, a kind that is new to the earth. This is the pleasure that comes from releasing yourself from competition and the games of superior and inferior and looking with new eyes on all that surrounds you.

Hierarchy has its pleasures, or at least its satisfactions, especially if you find yourself on top. Before the democratic age—the age Whitman wants to inaugurate—this was common knowledge. It was delicious to be on high, looking down at the mass of unimproved humanity below. But those in the middle regions and even the lower orders could take satisfactions from a world based on order and degree. You knew who you were and where you stood. You knew what was valuable—it was what your masters affirmed. You knew what to reject and even repudiate, though often it was qualities possessed by yourself and those close to you.

You always knew where you stood—with other people, of course, but also with God. When John Milton created his version of heaven, it was intensely hierarchical: every angel knows its standing. Are you a throne, a dominion, a power, or simply an everyday seraphim? The unwillingness to accept heavenly hierarchy was integral to Satan's rebellion and integral to Milton's sense of sin overall. In Milton's great poem, just relations of superior and inferior make life worth living. Milton was not alone in thinking so. Whitman wants to open a new world of democratic equality against the background of hierarchical ways of thought and social organization. He's come on the scene to displace John Milton and his kind, offering an American alternative to them.

Whitman found much to admire in the literary classics. He read Chaucer and Dante with appreciation. But he came to believe that such writers—and indeed nearly all writers who came before him—were not directly relevant to the new American nation. Most past literature was *feudal*. Whitman wanted a new literature than was not about the rich, the powerful, and the glamorous but about everyday people, the people who made up the heart and sinews of the democracy. He speaks often in his prose works about the need to displace feudalism and to create a democratic literature. Up until his present moment, he believes, almost all literature has focused on the rich and powerful. We're asked to look up at them with awe and sometimes with envy. They are what fascinates. They are at the center of virtually all Western art. The cultural critic Paul Cantor effectively describes nineteenth-century America's lingering fascinating with feudalism: "Once the United States set itself up as a democracy, Americans perversely began yearning to recapture something of the old aristocratic aura. Virtually from the moment Americans chose to split off from England, they fell into the grip of Anglophilia, deriving much of their culture—their literature, their music, their painting, their architecture—from English sources. The patriotic hymn to US liberty, 'My Country 'Tis of Thee,' is paradoxically sung to the tune of England's 'God Save the King'" (p. 23).

Whitman brooded on Shakespeare all through his life. He recognized Shakespeare's consummate artistry and his ability to give pleasure and instruction. Walt loved to go to the theater and took in Shakespeare plays whenever he could. But he was unhappy with what he saw as Shakespeare's fixation on kings and queens and nobility. In time, Walt came to think that Shakespeare's take on the aristocracy was highly critical. (Which it is. Even Henry V, whom Shakespeare appears to celebrate, has his dark side, and it is not easy to find an entirely admirable monarch in all the plays.) In time, Walt came to suggest that Shakespeare had cleared the way for democratic writing by subtly demystifying the nobility. In an essay on Shakespeare's history plays, Whitman writes, "Will it not indeed be strange if the author of 'Othello' and 'Hamlet' is destined to live in America, in a generation or two, less as the cunning draughtsman of the passions, and more as putting on record the full expose . . . of the political theory and results, or the reason-why and necessity for them which America has come on earth to abnegate and replace" (LoA, p. 1150).

Shakespeare, Whitman feels, has written an "expose" of feudalism that helps justify the American experiment

Whitman wants to create new forms of writing that render everyday people. He's interested in depicting the average, the commonplace. To him, the true poet is nothing but the emanation of the people. His task is to celebrate them and let them know how splendid they truly are. Whitman liked to think of himself as an average and everyday person—he felt that was part of what allowed him to represent the common people so well. In his life, for what it may be worth, Whitman had little time for rich people and politicians and businessmen. He liked the company of stage drivers, mechanics, farmers, bargemen, seamstresses, nurses, and mothers of big families. He lived a non- and antifeudal life.

As the poem unfolds, Whitman encounters more obstacles on his way to completing his vision of a democracy. He has to deal with sex, with God and with Jesus, with his own status as a poet and the future of his influence. Oddly enough, he's going to have to fight it out with the sun. He'll need to explore the part that violence plays in democracy, and he'll have to confront death again. But now that he's united Self and Soul, created the metaphor of the grass, and offered his first panoptic vision of America, Walt Whitman is on the move.

THESE STATES

All through Whitman's work, he refers to America as "these states." He's in love with these states. The thought of them overwhelms him with pleasure and pride. In *Song of Myself*, he calls America "the nation of many nations" (l. 330) and in that phrase captures a strong quotient of his joy in democracy. He's "a southerner soon as a northerner," which is something to say in the year 1855 (l. 331).

Whitman tells us, "I am . . . a Yankee bound my own way" (l. 332). "A Kentuckian walking the vale of the Elkhorn in my deerskin leggings" (l. 333),

> A boatman over the lakes or bays or along coasts . . . . a Hoosier, a Badger, a Buckeye,
> A Lousianian or Georgian, a poke-easy from sandhills and pines.
> (ll. 334–335)

He's at home in Canada too, which Whitman no doubt hoped would in time merge with the states.

At home in the hills of Vermont or the woods of Maine or a Texas ranch, he's a "comrade of Californians . . . . comrade of free northwesterners, loving their big proportions" (l. 339).

Whitman returns to the theme of these states in the poem and throughout his work. He's particularly disposed to sew North and South together, reminding his contemporaries that so far—so far—they are one. And of course Whitman hopes that will continue, though the jeopardy is great.

Whitman tells us again and again how different the states are. They are like separate nations. In the preface to *Leaves*, he speaks of "the practical acknowledgement of the citizens of one state by the citizens of all other states" (LoA, p. 6). When we meet someone, however casually, we want to know: Where are you from? Which state is yours?

Most of us feel a strong if rarely spoken affinity for the state we were born in. It's home, and we imbibe its customs and mores with pleasure. But then and now, you can know from early in life that your birth state is not your true state, not the place that matches your spirit. So away you go to Texas or Alabama or Ohio or California and set yourself down in a place that's almost as different from your Maine or your Vermont as another nation. And this new nation happens also to be yours.

It's often said, and there is little doubt that Whitman would approve, that the true New Yorkers, the ones who have the strongest claim to a life in Manhattan or Brooklyn or Queens, are not always the ones born there. It's those who, often beginning early, pine for the life of the ultimate American city. They come for the commerce or the art; they come because their sexuality only fits a big, roaring metropolis; they come for ambition; or they come for the sort of privacy that great cities can in their way provide. They come to be free and to be at home.

So a young girl born on the Upper East Side of Manhattan can begin pining early for the plains, the mountains, for horses and the freedom of grand open spaces. Off she goes to Wyoming, to North or South Dakota. And there she's happy—the state resonates with her spirit.

Over time these states have established potent identities. They protect and affirm those who are born to them, and they beckon those whose hearts yearn for such places as they are. Is there any nation in the world where there is so much regional difference as there is in America?

This invigorating difference comes with dangers. The states that are nearly nations in themselves always have the potential to break apart and even to fly into warfare. It happened once, in 1861. The chances of its happening again are real.

That is all the more reason to stress the unity of the states as well as their singularity. Different as we are, we are one: bound together by our commitment to liberty and equality and our belief in the pursuit of happiness for all. That's why Whitman can pass serenely from one state to the next, at least in the zones of his imagination. He can be that Kentuckian in leggings, stalking game; a Yankee trader; "a Hoosier, a Badger, a Buckeye"—a person from Indiana, Wisconsin, or Ohio. The states compete with each other now as they did then—now in elections, through sports, in commerce and art. Fifty nations, each a star on the flag: fifty nations that are absolutely singular in their identities, but fifty nations that, through their commitment to freedom and democracy, compose one.

SONGS OF TRIUMPH

As Whitman nears the midpoint of his poem, he chants a series of triumphal songs. And why shouldn't he? Emerson had looked out into the country and asked for an American bard. He wanted one who could take in the national expanse. "Our logrolling, our stumps and their politics, our fisheries, our Negroes, and Indians, our boasts and our repudiations, the wrath of rogues, and the pusillanimity of honest men, the northern trade, the southern planting, the Western clearing, Oregon, and Texas, are yet unsung" (LoA, p. 465). Whitman has begun to sing them—and he's done more.

He's composed a portrait of himself as an average American, an American Self—and symbolically stripped it down. He's voided it of cultural accumulations. Then he's made contact with his Soul, depicted it in all its sensitivity and charm. Outrageously enough, he's dramatized the carnal connection of Self and Soul. From there the world of imagination's opened up to him. His vision has become intense and mobile—he sees with preternatural power, from the "spirit of God" to the "mossy scabs of the worm-fence, and heaped stones, and elder and mullen and pokeweed" (l. 89). Then, perhaps his greatest triumph of imagination so far, he's hit on the metaphor of the grass—a trope that concentrates the right relation between individual and group. He's expanded the circle of American inclusion with the lonely young woman, the runaway slave, the trapper and his bride, and the Black plowman. He's launched his tour through the democracy, looking down on men and women of all sorts, savoring their experience, hymning common life, pulling us together, and guarding us from loneliness. And last, Whitman's offered his paean to the states with their stunning beauty and variety. Why shouldn't he crow a little?

Walt has a long way to go in filling out his vision for America and of Americans. There's still a lot to contend with: death (once again), God and Jesus (the whole history of religion, in fact), violence, sex, and (strangely enough) the sun. But now is the time for some celebration. Closing in on the middle of the poem, Walt looks back and records his triumphs:

I am the poet of the body,
And I am the poet of the soul.

The pleasures of heaven are with me, and the pains of hell are
    with me,
The first I graft and increase upon myself . . . . the latter I translate
    into a new tongue.
I am the poet of the woman the same as the man,
And I say it is as great to be a woman as to be a man,
And I say there is nothing greater than the mother of men.

I chant a new chant of dilation or pride,
We have had ducking and deprecating about enough,
I show that size is only development. (ll. 422–431)

Walt is the poet of body and soul, and he shows us what the conjunction of the two can reveal about American promise. He knows something new about pleasure and pain and something that should have been understood forever about the status of women and the status of men. He chants a chant of confidence as well, confidence in this new nation, this America.

Soon Walt has reached the apogee of his democratic pride—and he does something dramatic to signify it. Remember that the author's name doesn't appear on the cover of the 1855 *Leaves,* nor is it in the book's opening pages. It's not until nearly midway through that Walt feels sure enough about what he's achieved to speak it:

Walt Whitman, an American, one of the roughs, a kosmos,
Disorderly fleshy and sensual . . . . eating drinking and breeding,
No sentimentalist . . . . no stander above men and women or apart
    from them . . . . no more modest than immodest. (ll. 499–501)

"Walt Whitman, an American, one of the roughs, a kosmos." Surely one of the best and most memorable lines in the poem: it signifies his fealty to the old roughneck identity, but adds on, rather charmingly, that this roughneck is also a kosmos—a spiritual universe. (Years later, when Walt was trying to secure government work in Washington, DC, Senator Salmon P. Chase of Ohio moved to deny him, in part because he had admitted to being "one of the roughs"; of Whitman's identity as "a kosmos," Senator Chase made no mention [Epstein, p. 204].) Walt the roughneck-shaman is ascendant.

"Walt Whitman, an American": maybe Walt hasn't been an American up until this point, at least by his own lights. Maybe as he sees it, you're not an American until you can be tender and tough at once, revel in imagining yourself as a blade of grass, and happily install yourself in a catalogue of equals and friends. Maybe Walt feels that he's the first true American. Outrageous? Maybe. But as we've seen, and will see, Walt is nothing if not daring and confident. I'm not sure there has ever been a more fearless poet.

Walt steps forward boldly now in the knowledge that he's achieving a new form of being and that he's done poetic work worth doing:

Unscrew the locks from the doors!
Unscrew the doors themselves from their jambs!

Whoever degrades another degrades me . . . . and whatever is done
    or said returns at last to me,
And whatever I do or say I also return.

Through me the afflatus surging and surging . . . . through me the
    current and index.

I speak the password primeval . . . . I give the sign of democracy;
By God! I will accept nothing which all cannot have their
    counterpart of on the same terms. (ll. 502–508)

Walt is echoing Jesus here. Says the teacher, whatever you do unto the least of mine, you do also to me. But Walt is more boisterous about it.

Unscrew the locks from the doors, so that I, Walt Whitman an American, can be sure that no one is being degraded. And if anyone is—well, this rowdy, rambunctious fella may do something about it. This is Walt's first appearance as what we might call American Jesus; in this case, he's akin to Jesus in the temple snapping his whip at the money lenders.

Unscrew the locks from the doors! One hallmark of the true progressive is skepticism about boundaries. Walt doesn't want to tear down every wall and border. But he wants to remove, or at least attenuate, the divisions between women and men, Black and White, old and young, humans and animals, humanity and nature. The conservative is far more responsive to borders. He believes that age-old distinctions are there for a reason and that it's a good idea to err on the side of caution. "Good fences make good neighbors," Robert Frost's country-bred farmer in "Mending Wall" says. Taken too far, the progressive's resistance to boundaries can lead to painful disorder, even chaos. The conservative's affection for rules and boundaries can become suffocating. At his worst, he devolves into an angry man at a massive rally, chanting about building more walls.

Overall, this is a triumphal passage. Walt is reveling in his achievement and celebrating himself full out. Soon he'll be going back into what William Blake would call mental fight. But for now, he's chanting his triumphs. Serious encounters are on the way. But first, one more blissful interlude.

POET OF THE BODY

First-time readers of Whitman who love him immediately usually aren't thinking much about his democratic philosophy or his vision of America present and to come.

They fall in love with something else in *Song of Myself,* and that's Walt's joy in being alive. The poem is a hymn to vitality and the pleasure of existence. Walt gives thanks for the world as he finds it. He's an unqualified lover of natural beauty and a lover of the body. One of his chief impulses is gratitude. Walt is like one of the Buddhist sages who is full of thanks, though there is no being to whom he obviously owes it. Walt finds himself lucky, very lucky, to be alive.

The philosopher ponders the question, Why is there something instead of nothing at all? The poet looks out into the teeming world and, without pondering the why at any great length, celebrates the simple fact of being. Walt contemplates the bending of his thumb joint and is filled with awe at what he sees. He tells us that "a mouse is miracle enough to stagger sextillions of infidels" (l. 668). (And he is right.) As we edge our way to the thematic center of the poem and the crisis that comes with it, Walt offers a love hymn to his own body. "If I worship any particular thing," says Walt, "it shall be some of the spread of my body":

> Breast that presses against other breasts it shall be you,
> My brain it shall be your occult convolutions,
> Root of washed sweet-flag, timorous pond snipe, nest of guarded
>   duplicate eggs, it shall be you.
> Mixed tussled hay of head and beard and brawn it shall be you.
>   (ll. 534–537)

Breast, mind, genitals, hair, and muscle: it's all miracle, and Walt worships it as such. ("Sweet flag" is the phallically formed calamus plant; the pond snipe generally has two eggs in the nest.) Is this passage narcissistic? Some would say so. But narcissism is nothing more than self-love that has become pathological—a cause of suffering to oneself and others. Like Percy Bysshe Shelley, Whitman believes that love of the self is a necessary part of sane and whole being. And face it—the human form is a miracle: there is no reason not to fall in love with it.

In Whitman's time there was prudishness about the body and fear of its power to yield pleasure. Have we overcome all that? Perhaps we have. Now, though, we seek physical perfection: we must be firm, youthful, unscarred, unblemished, fat free. Whitman waves all that away. The body—your body—is a marvel. Love and admire. Worship freely. "There is that lot of me," the amply proportioned poet says, "and all so luscious" (l. 545).

Note the key word "worship" in Walt's hymn to his body. Just because we democratic men and women have moved away from conventional religion, it doesn't mean that we can't experience awe and thanksgiving. All of the best impulses of religion—and there are plenty of them— remain for us to appropriate and enjoy, though often in a new and slightly unfamiliar form.

THE SUN

At the end of Whitman's hymn to physical life, he tells us that he's willing to worship the sun. "Sun so generous it shall be you" (SoM, l. 539). In the 1855 preface, he compares the sun to the compassionate poet's broad powers of acceptance in one of the most beautiful lines he ever wrote: the poet "judges not as the judge judges but as the sun falling around a helpless thing" (LoA, p. 9). Often throughout the poem, Whitman has an affectionate relation with the sun. But not always. In a poem that affirms almost everything in creation, there are a few images, a few figures, that Whitman regards ambivalently. There are schoolteachers; there are contemporary preachers; there are literary men; and there are the past promulgators of religious doctrine. Whitman doesn't *hate* any of these people out and out. Whitman isn't a hater. But he does regard them complexly: he doesn't feel the unalloyed affection for them that he feels for others, especially working men and women.

Whitman seems to love every aspect of the natural world, without qualification, every aspect but one. He sometimes (not always) finds the sun to be a distressing, even an inimical force.

Few are the writers who launch vendettas against King Sol. Ahab says that he'd strike the sun if it insulted him, but the enmity doesn't seem terribly specific—he might as well have said that he'd strike heaven. Whitman, though, is bothered by the sun. He casts an aspersion here and an aspersion there. At one point, he announces that "there are millions of suns left" (l. 26), suggesting that the sun is not unique and uniquely important. At another time, he speaks of "the suns I see and the suns I cannot see" (l. 351), multiplying the sun again and so diminishing it a bit.

But at about the middle of the poem, he becomes serious about his opposition to the sun. Here the contention between Walt and the sun seems an issue of life or death. When Whitman describes the sunrise, he describes a struggle:

> Something I cannot see puts upward libidinous prongs,
> Seas of bright juice suffuse heaven.
>
> The earth by the sky staid with . . . . the daily close of their junction,
> The heaved challenge from the east that moment over my head,
> The mocking taunt, See then whether you shall be master!
>   (ll. 557–561)

The sun is rising in the east, and rather than greeting it as a friend or brother, Whitman falls into a competition with it. "See then whether you shall be master": one assumes that is Whitman talking, not the sun. The poet fears being overpowered and dominated by the sun. Why? How could the brilliant, fructifying sun be an enemy to Walt?

Clearly we are witnessing a power struggle. Mastery is at stake here: and accordingly all of Whitman's strong feelings about domination and submission come into play. Remember, Whitman hates abasement in all forms. "Dazzling and tremendous," he says,

> how quick the sunrise would kill me,
> If I could not now and always send sunrise out of me. (ll. 562–563)

Whitman needs to send sunrise out of him so as not to perish, literally or metaphorically, from the presence of the early-morning sun.

Why does the sun bother Whitman as much as it does? Why does the sun seem to present itself as a figure of opposition—what Northrop Frye would call a blocking agent—in the quest to create American democracy and give birth to men and women of genuinely egalitarian temper?

Kings and pharaohs often find their emblems in the sun, affirming it as the sign of unified imperial power. It is one, isolated and alone, and it is so magnificent that it can compel worship. (Shakespeare's King Richard II compares himself directly to the sun; Prince Hal, soon to be Henry V, and a shrewder statesman by far, affirms his power to "imitate the sun.")

I suspect that to Whitman, the sun is an image for royal power and for the feudalism he hopes to displace. The sun is isolated and potent. It seems to rule the universe. It can stand as an emblem for absolutist, patriarchal rule.

One of the first-written poems to appear in the 1855 *Leaves of Grass* would in time be called "A Boston Ballad." It's not one of Walt's best, far from it; but it's that uncommon instance in Whitman, a poem that's overarchingly negative. When Walt writes critically, he usually reveals something about the heart of his project.

In "Boston Ballad," the old heroes of the American Revolution rise from their graves to attend a celebratory parade in the middle of Boston. Here they come:

> The old graveyards of the hills have hurried to see;
> Uncountable phantoms gather by flank and rear of it,
> Cocked hats of mothy mold and crutches made of mist,
> Arms in slings and old men leaning on young men's shoulders.
>   (LoA, p. 135)

The old campaigners are shocked at their grandsons on parade, so orderly, well-dressed, and smart. The celebration they've come to see has an authoritarian air to it: the president's marshal is there, with the dragoons and cannons and the federal foot soldiers. The old soldiers hate it, and run for the hills, run back to their graves. They detest the new imperial America. It's not what they fought for, not what they were wounded and died for. The nation is no longer theirs.

These, we may presume, are the New England soldiers, the ones who fought and lost their lives at Concord and Lexington and at Breeds Hill, in the conflict that would eventually be called the Battle of Bunker Hill. It was there, just a few miles from the site of Whitman's parade, that the American Revolution genuinely began.

This was the start of the first successful anti-imperialist rebellion the world had seen. People stood up to a powerful colonial oppressor and got the better of it. They made a lasting statement.

What happened to the spirit of June 1775? What makes "Boston Ballad" a tragedy, not a celebration of America's revolutionary tradition? In Whitman's poem, the people have no time for the old campaigners on celebration day. Americans are now in love with spit and polish, parades and the parade marshals. They've lost the democratic spirit of their ancestors.

What do they really want? What do they deserve? Whitman knows. His Boston compatriots would be altogether delighted, the poet says, if across the water they patched together the remains of King George III and sent him to America to rule and receive proper reverence. So exhume him from the earth and bundle his bones into a coffin, fuse what you can, and this above all—put a crown on the old, mad tyrant's head. "Clap the skull on top of the ribs, and clap a crown on top of the skull" (LoA, p. 137). Then the new generation of Americans, who have forgotten about what their forebears achieved on the bloody hill a few years before, can do what they pine to do: fall down and worship their king. "The crown is come to its own and more than its own" (p. 137).

The implication is clear. When you forget who the revolutionaries were, what they fought for, and what they fought against, you are in danger of lapsing back into the old ways—the way of kings. Whitman took seriously, very seriously, the idea that we in America were creating a new order of the world. We were moving into a fresh phase of history, when obeisance to kings and nobles, the rich and the glamourous, would end. We wouldn't worship god or kings, but save our reverence for one another, a community of equals bound by friendship, affection, and the strongly held view that no one should ever bow to anyone else. In 1855, we were at a point of potential transition, Whitman thought: we could make the move from one era to the next. And we'd do so—Whitman was not overwhelmingly modest—guided by the privately published, eccentrically printed book of an uneducated, non- and antielite poet. Whitman knew the danger of sliding back into feudalism was always there, and he hoped to save us from it with poems like *Song of Myself* and "Boston Ballad."

The worship of the king, the sun, or the sun-like figure, is always a temptation in a democracy. What democratic citizens often fear most is chaos. The sight of equal people going about their business, pursuing their desires and their goals, can seem chaotic to some of us. And in a society where there is no stable ruling class and few enduring structures of power, chaos always *is* a real possibility. You can solve that problem in a number of ways. You can reaffirm the personal bonds of the democracy. You can remind people, as Whitman liked to do, that they are involved in what is probably the greatest and most promising social venture of all time and that it requires vigilance and hard work. But you can also try to resolve social chaos, or the threat of chaos, in another way. You can turn in the direction of a potent figure of authority. You can confirm a king, a god-like man (usually it *is* a man) who gives laws, who affirms values, who is clear and precise and declarative. You can find a man who stands to the nation as the sun stands to the solar system.

This is the sort of person Freud describes in *Group Psychology.* The leader, he says, need love no one; he is the perfect narcissist, completely self-confident and self-absorbed. He may doubt others and undermine them for his purposes, but he never doubts himself, at least not publicly. Says Freud, "His intellectual acts were strong and independent even in isolation, and his will needed no reinforcement from others. . . . His ego had few libidinal ties; he loved no one but himself, or other people only in so far as they served his needs. To objects his ego gave away no more than was necessary" (*Standard Edition,* vol. 18, p. 123). He preyed—and still does—on the weakness of the group. "The members of a group stand in need of the illusion that they are equally and justly loved by their leader; but the leader himself need love no one else, he may be of a masterful nature, absolutely narcissistic, self-confident and independent" (pp. 123–124). For we know, Freud says, that "love puts a check upon narcissism" (p. 124). All this Whitman understood. Though of course the question remained: What would Walt do with and about his own aspirations to leadership?

The leader's arrival sometimes comes as a relief. When the world seems to be passing out of control, we want nothing so much as stability. And sun-like men can bring it, though at a cost.

In *The Republic,* Plato describes how democracy becomes unmanageable: people cannot live on happily doing exactly what they like. They will drown in private and public disorder. So in time along comes the savior, who strides forward to affirm balance and propriety. What Plato does not understand, Whitman might say, is that in a true democracy, American democracy, people can achieve stability by making strong and flexible the bonds that hold them together. We'll have the committed whole that we create, so we won't need the enforced totality that the sun offers.

Faced by the sun, or by sun-like figures, Whitman has an overt strategy. He proclaims that he's just as strong and fierce as the sun itself.

"We also ascend dazzling and tremendous as the sun, / We found our own my soul in the calm and cool of the daybreak" (SoM, ll. 564–565). Walt ascends with all the force of a king or lord—he's a democratic man. How could he not? All of his democratic contemporaries might do likewise, matching force with force.

But there's an implicit strategy of rebuttal to the sun, too: Think of the grass! Remember that you are one blade, and that can at times be lonely and confusing. But you are also more than that. You are part of the great green expanse: you belong, you're one of us. You don't need a sun-king to help you feel at home on the earth. You don't need an overbearing god-man to create order for you. The order is there in the totality of the grass. The grass is the master metaphor in the poem that subtly opposes the metaphor of the sun.

Another way to put it: the sun gives you only unity, for it masters everything it shines on. The grass gives you both unity (its entire expanse) and diversity (in its individual blades). Oddly enough, one of the best analogues to Whitman's grass is what Jacques Derrida calls *différance*. By *différance*, I take Derrida to refer to the ever-expanding field of written words in a text, multiple in their associations, ever generative of further meanings, and antithetical to closure and resolution. There is, it seems to me, a democratic ethos in Derrida's thinking. However, unlike Whitman's grass, Derrida's renowned master trope, *différance*, only affirms diversity, endless diversity; there is no principle of unity to enter into dialectical relation with the free play of signifiers. The genius of Whitman's grass metaphor is that it works both ways, unifying and individualizing at once. But we need to live up to the difficult terms of the trope—balancing both sides of our identities with skill and care.

Look out for the sun! Or so Whitman tells us. It's not enough simply to read Walt's poem and to understand why the sun is so mesmerizingly potent. The work demands more. In a democracy, Walt suggests, we have to be vigilant about our hunger for kings. Just having read about that hunger isn't enough. We need to look into our hearts and gaze out into the culture, and when we see the sun begin to rise, we need to step up and respond. Even if the sun-king concentrates ideas and impulses that we take to be just and necessary, we've got to reject him. The sun-king can tell all the truth in the world, but at the base, it's never true. He always embodies tyranny, and he always is our foe. So, when he rises, as he has and will, fight back, both internally and in the world at large. Fight back benevolently—and think of the grass.

Whitman was sometimes confident that a new age was beginning with the publication of *Leaves*. No more tyrants. No more sun worship. Mark Twain, a younger contemporary, who admired Walt and once went to hear him present his memories of President Lincoln, saw it differently. Twain was nearly as taken with the question of aristocracy and its relations to democratic life as Whitman was. Whitman usually gives aristocracy the silent treatment: the best way to dispose of it is to affirm something better. When he's not fighting the sun, or maligning Boston's hunger for King George, he's busy unfolding the pleasures and trials of democracy. Twain, on the other hand, is transfixed by feudalism and enjoys nothing so much as debunking it. He goes after King Arthur's Court in *A Connecticut Yankee*, the British monarchy in *The Prince and the Pauper*, pretensions to royalty all through *Huck Finn*, and the corruption of the nobility in *Personal Recollections of Joan of Arc*. But with the exception of the latter book, Twain's writing about kings and dukes tends to be comic. He sends up royalist pretensions, yes, but he doesn't have a blood vendetta against them. He dislikes "the quality," as Huck calls them, but he doesn't care for crowds and crowd mentality either.

Twain's view of the aristocracy is far more urbane than Whitman's. He's content to satirize it, and one imagines he would have been happy to do so for decades on end. He once observed, "It is a saddening thought but we cannot change our nature—we are all alike, we human beings; and in our blood and bone, and ineradicable, we carry the seeds out of which monarchies and aristocracies are grown: worship of gauds, titles, distinction, power. We have to worship these things and their possessors, we are all born so, and we cannot help it. We have to be despised by somebody whom we regard as above us, or we are not happy, we have to have somebody to worship and envy or we cannot be content" (*Autobiography*, vol. 2, p. 314). To Twain as to Freud, love of authority lies deep in the human heart. There really is no way around it. It will be back again and again, and the best defense is to laugh it temporarily away. Walt invites us to imagine a time when aristocracy leaves the world, replaced by the love of equal comrades.

Isn't Whitman coming on as something of a god-man in this poem, a sun himself? He does, after all, claim to be "a kosmos," and much more besides. And what about other figures who aspire to achieve some measure of greatness in America? Maybe in democracy we have to do without them entirely. Whitman will take this matter up before the poem ends, posing the question of greatness and influence quite explicitly and offering imaginative response. But he may offer his best response beyond the poem, in the realm of day-to-day experience. Before that, however, he has further to go in unfolding his vision.

Whitman's next major scene of passage is surely the strangest in the poem. It depicts a sexual encounter, and one far more fraught than the joyous tumble that Self and Soul took.

THE GENERATIVE GOD

I s this then a touch," Whitman asks, "quivering me to a new identity?"
(SoM, l. 618). It's clear soon that the touch is Whitman's own and its
object is himself. He is, it seems irrefutable, putting his fingers or hands
to his penis: but he does not find this a comfortable experience, not at all.

> Flames and ether make a rush for my veins,
> Treacherous tip of me reaching and crowding to help them,
> My flesh and blood playing out lightning, to strike what is hardly
>   different from myself,
> On all sides prurient provokers stiffening my limbs,
> Straining the udder of my heart for its withheld drip,
> Behaving licentious toward me, taking no denial,
> Depriving me of my best as for a purpose,
> Unbuttoning my clothes and holding me by the bare waist,
> Deluding my confusion with the calm of the sunlight and pasture
>   fields,
>
> Immodestly sliding the fellow-senses away. (ll. 619–628)

The passage is oddly both evasive and graphic: we may think we know
what's going on, but the language is highly figurative and often indirect.
Who is seducing whom? Is it the Self and Soul in action again? Probably
not. That tumble was voluntary, and seemed joyous. This one is highly
fraught and anything but simply and directly pleasurable. Where are we?
What's unfolding? And who are those "prurient provokers" bothering
the poet?

All Whitman's senses have gone into remission, except for touch, which is dominating him completely. (We might say, not quite in good taste, that Whitman is raping himself.) His other senses are arrayed against Whitman, or passively watching the scene unfold.

> They bribed to swap off with touch, and go and graze at the edges
>   of me,
> No consideration, no regard for my draining strength or my anger,
> Fetching the rest of the herd around to enjoy them awhile,
> Then all uniting to stand on a headland and worry me. (ll. 629–632)

"My anger." Why is Whitman so angry? He clearly does not want to engage in this act. He's distressed. It seems that he has been abandoned by all of his defenses, all of his ethical principles. They have deserted their posts, and now they stand on the headland, where they seem to be judging Whitman for what he's doing, but not preventing him from doing it. The "sentries," Whitman's trope for inhibitions or defenses, are not helping him out of his crisis—in time they seem to be cheering it on. Whitman's defenses have been converted into aids to desire.

> The sentries desert every other part of me,
> They have left me helpless to a red marauder,
> They all come to the headlands to witness and assist against me.
>   (ll. 633–635)

A red marauder! It seems that Walt has compounded his penis with a marauding tribesman. The sentries are gone, and now Whitman will do what he is both driven to do and fears doing.

> I am given up by traitors;
> I talk wildly . . . . I have lost my wits . . . . I and nobody else am the
>   greatest traitor,
> I went myself first to the headland . . . . my own hands carried me
>   there. (ll. 636–638)

Whitman is on the verge of ejaculation. There's a shift now in the value of "the headlands," which seems to be a visionary place, a sacred zone, perhaps a little like Delphi, where, sometimes at a cost, you go to find illumination.

Finally, Whitman gives in and gives up. "Unclench your floodgates!" (l. 640), he cries, as though he were commanding what's now compulsory. Unclench your floodgates! Reluctantly, even angrily, Whitman is going along with what's inevitably coming to pass.

What he's doing is clearly forbidden to him. His resistances have been overwhelmed, and he is no doubt expecting some kind of punishment or pain. The discourse against masturbation was strong during Whitman's time. And Whitman, open and accepting poet that he is, seems to have potent resistances to his own pleasure. It is not easy for many of us to embrace pleasure, especially of an erotic sort. We resist it, often for no terribly good reason. Whitman has been the victim of the strictures of his age, and it is hard for him to break through. In fact, he has to be overwhelmed into acquiescence and finally to passionate assent. "Unclench your floodgates!"

What's next? I suspect that Walt expects punishment of some kind, or at least a strong surge of guilt, maybe a crippling dose that makes him unable to continue on in his vision-quest. He's broken a law, perhaps, and now has to pay. But that's not how it goes.

> Blind loving wrestling touch! Sheathed hooded sharptoothed touch!
> Did it make you ache so leaving me? (ll. 641–642)

The tone has changed. Now Whitman is mild and understanding. His orgasm was pleasurable and painful both, and he's comforting himself about the experience. There really was nothing to worry about:

> Parting tracked by arriving . . . . perpetual payment of the perpetual loan,
> Rich showering rain, and recompense richer afterward.
> (ll. 643–644)

The rain of semen has fallen to the ground: but no punishment or tragedy has followed. Instead a new world comes into bloom, much as it did when the Egyptian god Atum spread his seed into space and brought worlds into being:

> Sprouts take and accumulate . . . . stand by the curb prolific and vital,
> Landscapes projected masculine full-sized and golden. (ll. 645–646)

What seemed sinful turns out the be richly fertilizing. Where there was resistance and confusion, now there is quiet pleasure.

There's no reason, Whitman appears to say, to fear or condemn unharmful pleasures; there's no reason to be in thrall to needless confinement. Democracy doesn't have to be all about public meetings and mass applause and walking the streets and saluting everyone you see. It can also be about private pleasures, in this case perhaps the most private of pleasures. The sun may look down on you, the defenses may turn into jeering multitudes, but you can make it through and carve a new path to joy. What comes after Whitman's interlude is tranquility, not quite the peace that passes understanding but a certain calm that will be the basis for more poems: a new thresholds for new departures into the future. "All truths wait in all things" (l. 647), says Walt; and now his journey continues, and he can find for us and for himself some more of those truths.

One might speculate that the reasons for Whitman's distress in the masturbation scene are multiple. I think it's possible that he's distressed by the fact that some, or even all, of the figures he's fantasizing about when he masturbates are male. Whitman's poetry is homoerotic from end to end. But when an admirer asked him in a letter if he wasn't a poet of active genital homosexuality, Whitman drew back, horrified and angry. The tone of his rebuttal to John Addington Symonds suggests that the possibility had never occurred to him. Could a poet as subtle and self-inquiring as Whitman never have thought about the possibility of homosexual sex? For a poet who says he'll tell us all, Whitman leaves many mysteries, and the mystery of his sexual life, as poet and man, is one of the most perplexing.

Another aspect of Whitman's distress in the masturbation scene comes, I suspect, from fear of stasis and fear of exclusivity. Walt's persona in the poem is the rambler, always on the move, connecting with person after person, but never being absorbed and fixed by any one. He claims to have had thousands of lovers. That claim doesn't scare or bother him. But if he took one lover, just one, that would fix him to a single object. And that would be so even if the lover were to be none other than himself.

Whitman wants, maybe above all things, not to be sun-like, for the sun is unity without diversity. Walt loves unity—the unity of these states in particular—but he will not purchase unity through forced homogeneity. When he stops with himself to find his own pleasure, there's a fear, I think, that he'll never get moving again. At the close of the masturbation scene, Whitman seems delighted to find that he can free himself. His fructifying semen is a trope for the new worlds and new people and new truths he will discover now that his sexual interlude is over. There are more poems to be written, more words to come. The interlude recharges Whitman's visionary energies instead of freezing them. He's ready to take on fresh obstacles and enjoy new pleasures. He'll soon be, as he likes to put it, afoot with his visions.

Maybe the most important aspect of this scene involves Walt's relations with his readers. See, the passage seems to say, there's nothing I won't tell you about myself. I'm willing to be completely vulnerable, completely open. Has any other major writer made himself as susceptible to mockery as Whitman does in this scene? Masturbation: everyone does it, but no one talks about it. Well, not quite: there is Walt Whitman. He's coming at the reader undisguised and naked and easily ridiculed. It may be that masturbation is Walt's characteristic sexual mode, maybe the only mode he can engage in with success. "To touch my person to some one else's is about as much as I can stand" (l. 617), he says. Maybe, Walt hints, he's not capable of heterosexual intercourse or homosexual intercourse either. Maybe this is all he can do, or is disposed to do.

"Even the president of the United States sometimes must have to stand naked," Bob Dylan, a Whitman descendant, says. But the president won't generally do so, not in public view. Yet here is our great hobo poet, doing just that.

Whitman offers us an implicit question: If I'm willing to go so far with candor and self-exposure, reader, won't you do something similar for me? Won't you open yourself up to my vision, much as I've opened myself to you? For we are brothers, are we not? We are brothers and sisters in the democracy. And to one another we are open, accepting, kind.

THE ANIMALS

Whitman is frightened in the erotic interlude: scared of his own desires and, one might speculate, scared of self-exposure. But now, he's broken through. He's overcome fears, and he becomes bolder, more provocative, and less eager to please. He's shown himself and shown the world or whatever part happens to be paying attention that he's not afraid of erotic self-revelation.

After the poem's midpoint, *Song of Myself* grows darker. Whitman is confident enough to bring out his harsher side, though he sometimes does so in indirect ways. A Jungian might say that Whitman begins to make contact with his Shadow, the part of the psyche that concentrates aggressions and fears. That may be a little strong—Whitman's dark side is never terribly dark, but after the autoerotic section, we do see a new aspect of the poet.

A brief passage directly after the masturbation crisis appears to be about animals and Whitman's affection for them. And it is, but it's about more than that too:

> I think I could turn and live awhile with the animals . . . . they
>   are so placid and self-contained,
> I stand and look at them sometimes half the day long.
>   (ll. 684–685)

The Whitman of *Song* enjoys hanging around and not doing much of anything, placid and self-contained. His Soul loves being "in and out of the game, and watching and wondering at it" (l. 70). So this is entirely consistent with Walt's past persona.

Then matters shift. Walt tells us that he loves the animals, not only for what they do but for what they don't:

> They do not sweat and whine about their condition,
> The do not lie awake in the dark and weep for their sins,
> They do not make me sick discussing their duty to God,
> Not one is dissatisfied . . . . not one is demented with the mania of owning things,
> Not one kneels to another nor to his kind that lived thousands of years ago,
> Not one is respectable or industrious over the whole earth.
>   (ll. 686–691)

We're not talking primarily about animals anymore. Walt's writing about some human qualities he doesn't especially care for, using animal contentment as a point of contrast.

Whitman doesn't like weepers and whiners—no surprise there. He's a poet of vital affirmations. And he doesn't care for Puritan contrition either—No to staying awake at night crying out for one's sins. Nor is he devoted to people who spend their time talking about their solemn duty to the Lord God. They tend to be tiresome, life hating, and hungry to dominate others. When Walt talks about how the animals refrain from kneeling to each other, he's taking a swipe at aristocracy. But his main target in the passage is conventional religion. Whitman loves religion—and he wants Americans to be the most religious people on earth. But religion is a matter of doing reverence to what authentically inspires awe in the present—not kneeling to other humans who lived far in the past. Subtly, by talking about not worshiping others of our kind, Whitman is doubting the divinity of Jesus. It's a first step on his way to a reconfiguration of Jesus on behalf of democracy.

As to being industrious and respectable: well we know by now, Whitman likes to loaf and enjoy himself. Nor does owning things mean much to him. He probably wouldn't have liked the fancy lingo Marx uses when he speaks of the "fetishism of commodities." But Walt would have known exactly what Marx meant. Whitman too resisted the inclination to imbue things with the significance of people and people with the significance of mere things.

Whitman is leveling his guns against pious, dutiful New England types steeped in self-regard. But the indictment reaches out to everyone who prefers middle-class respectability and self-congratulatory self-belittling to the pleasures of the earth and the joys of democracy. When you feel low and set apart, look at your fellow men and women and see what a miracle they are. Or immerse yourself in nature and take joy in the green world's presence in our lives. If you're going to worship anything, Whitman suggests all through the poem, you might consider worshiping nature, your body, and your fellow American citizens.

That sentiment comes through in an artful line that anticipates Whitman's use of the animals to brood on human smugness and fake piety. "The cow crunching with depressed head surpasses any statue" (l. 667), he says. Whitman has no affection for statues—they're residues of a past culture, when the people knelt in worship to the supposedly great and did not know their own dignity. That's changed or changing. A real democracy will have no need for statues that elevate individuals to deific status. A more truly democratic form might be the mural that shows the brothers and sisters in the democracy doing their work with dignity.

Whitman would have loved Diego Rivera's celebration of American autoworkers in his grand Detroit mural. Rivera, a visual artist, who may be among the truest of all Walt's twentieth- and twenty-first-century heirs, says in his autobiography, "The workers I had seen in Europe were brothers of the poor from whom sprang everything I have ever loved. Deep inside me I had discovered an enormous artistic reservoir. It was of the kind that had enabled the American genius Walt Whitman to create, on a grander scale than anyone had before, the poetry of the common people, working, suffering, fighting, seeking joy, living and dying" (p. 41).

WALT BECOMES OTHER

understand the large hearts of heroes" (SoM, l. 818), says Whitman. I think he has reason to say so. Whitman never fought in a war and never would, but in a spiritual sense, he's been brave. He's told us who he is and what he's about. He's been willing to make himself vulnerable in the sexual encounter of Self and Soul and more so in the autoerotic scene at the poem's midpoint. Walt's launched himself on a symbolic quest that might take him anywhere—and might well fail. Surely Whitman has been spiritually brave and heroically candid.

After the autoerotic crisis is resolved, Whitman offers his sharp polemic against the well-heeled, guilty, and industrious. But he also takes us on a tour of the nation. He ranges from ocean to ocean and everywhere in between, reminding us Americans how fortunate we are to live in the land we do. Its beauty and fertility astound. His imagination flies

Where the quail is whistling betwixt the woods and the wheatlot,
Where the bat flies in the July eve . . . . where the great goldbug
    drops through the dark;
Where the flails keep time on the barn floor,
Where the brook puts out of the roots of the old tree and flows to the
    meadow,
Where cattle stand and shake away flies with the tremulous
    shuddering of their hides,
Where the cheese-cloth hangs in the kitchen, and andirons straddle
    the hearth-slab, and cobwebs fall in festoons from the rafters;
Where triphammers crash . . . . where the press is whirling its
    cylinders;

Wherever the human heart beats with terrible throes out of its ribs.
  (ll. 731–738)

We can only be grateful for the amazing gift of the land and culture that surrounds us.

Whitman does something else remarkable after the central crisis of the poem: he doesn't just see and enumerate the people living our democratic life. He becomes them for protracted bouts: "I am the man . . . . I suffered . . . . I was there" (l. 827), he says. "I am the hounded slave" (l. 834), he writes. "I am an old artillerist, and tell of some fort's bombardment . . . . and am there again" (l. 853). He becomes a fireman fighting a dangerous fire. He's identified with people before, but rather glancingly. Now he's confident in his identifications, and he goes deeper. How does he gain this right? Why is it available to him now?

The fireman passage goes this way:

I am the mashed fireman with breastbone broken . . . . tumbling
    walls buried me in their debris,
Heat and smoke I inspired . . . . I heard the yelling shouts of my
    comrades,
I heard the distant click of their picks and shovels;
They have cleared the beams away . . . . they tenderly lift me forth.

I lie in the night air in my red shirt . . . . the pervading hush is for
    my sake,
Painless after all I lie, exhausted but not so unhappy,
White and beautiful are the faces around me . . . . the heads are
    bared of their fire-caps. (ll. 843–849)

There's an intense immediacy to this identification, a fullness. He's doing what he said he would, and most convincingly. "I pass death with the dying, and birth with the new-washed babe" (l. 124), he tells us, and in time he does.

D. H. Lawrence, who in many ways owed his poetic career to Whitman's inspiration, sneered at Whitman's powers of identification. He said that Walt was presumptuous in his belief that he could change places at will with anyone. But one might counter that Walt has earned the right:

he's come to know himself almost fully. In the Self and Soul conjunction and in the masturbation scene, he has, like the narrator of Stevens's "Tea at the Palaz of Hoon," found himself "more truly and more strange." And when you can do that, perhaps you can begin to understand others as well. Having achieved what he does in the onanism scene and the duel with the sun, Whitman now feels he has the imaginative and ethical power to deepen his identificatory poetics.

Does Walt succeed with these deep identifications? I think that overall he does. In the fireman passage, he captures the feel of risking life in a worthy cause and the camaraderie that ensues when working people band together to achieve something worthwhile. When the mashed foreman falls, his comrades surround him and offer the tribute of their beautifully sympathetic faces and their bared heads. Walt is one with the mashed foreman but also persuasively one with the firefighting team— or at least he seems so to me.

A MASSACRE

understand the large hearts of heroes" (SoM, l. 818). *Song of Myself* is in its way an epic, and like a true epic poet, Walt seeks to teach his readers what they need to know to live well. Homer taught his listeners how to pray, how to sacrifice, how to imagine the gods, and also, perhaps most important, what it means to be a martial hero. Those reading Whitman's poem for the first time might believe as they pass the midpoint that Walt will prove to be a pacifist. He loves all natural life, and he loves all (or almost all) men and women in the world. Why would he want to see anyone harmed?

Yet Whitman does not deny martial heroism. He sees it as essential for the development of the new democracy. Our heroism cannot be Homeric heroism, it goes without saying. We need a version of bravery that fits the new way of life.

"I tell not the fall of Alamo," says Walt, "not one escaped to tell the fall of Alamo, / The hundred and fifty are dumb yet at Alamo" (ll. 864–865). The scene from the Texas Revolution that Whitman does relate is the scene of a massacre of Texas fighters. Whitman says that no one exists to tell the story of the Alamo—at least no American. But I suspect that Whitman didn't want to write about the Alamo, and not only because it had been written about so often, even by 1855. Writing about the Alamo would have inevitably meant writing about heroes, the famous commanders whose statures are far above the hundred and fifty who died with them. He would have had to write about the colonels who commanded the fort, Colonel Travis, Colonel Bowie, and Colonel Davy Crockett, one of the most storied figures in American pioneer history. These are the sorts of men to whom people raise statues, and one recalls that to Whitman, contemplating a munching cow is more edifying than gazing at one of those.

Whitman wants a fresh slate. Instead of writing about the Alamo, he writes about the massacre of 412 young Texans at Goliad, in 1836. "They were," he says, "the glory of the race of rangers":

> Matchless with a horse, a rifle, a song, a supper or courtship,
> Large, turbulent, brave, handsome, generous, proud and
>   affectionate,
> Bearded, sunburnt, dressed in the free costume of hunters,
> Not a single one over thirty years of age. (ll. 873–876)

The rangers have fought furiously against their enemies, Walt says. They've killed twice their number before they run out of ammunition and treat for honorable surrender. Terms are given, but the enemy reneges and takes the rangers out to slaughter:

> The second Sunday morning they were brought out in squads and
>   massacred . . . . it was beautiful early summer,
> The work commenced about five o'clock and was over by eight.
>   (ll. 877–878)

Whitman's heroes are not victors—they've lost their fight. It's in their deaths that their heroism lies.

The scene of the massacre is horrifying:

> Some made a mad and helpless rush . . . . some stood stark and
>   straight,
> A few fell at once, shot in the temple or heart . . . . the living and
>   dead lay together,
> The maimed and mangled dug in the dirt . . . . the new-comers saw
>   them there;
> Some half-killed attempted to crawl away,
> These were dispatched with bayonets or battered with the blunts of
>   muskets;
> A youth not seventeen years old seized his assassin till two more
>   came to release him,

The three were all torn, and covered with the boy's blood.
    (ll. 880–886)

The Texans aren't victors but victims of deception and cruelty. Here is no celebration of victory—there's no victory to celebrate. Whitman doesn't gesture ahead to the culmination of the rebellion, which leads to the independence of Texas from Mexico and eventually to its becoming one of the states.

Why did Whitman choose this brutal, potentially dispiriting event? He tells us before the narrative of the slaughter itself begins. The rangers have been brought out, and it's clear to them what's about to happen. They are told by their enemies to abase themselves, but they will not. "None obeyed the command to kneel" (l. 879), Whitman writes. They would not grovel before their captors. True Americans, as Whitman says in the preface, have the air "of persons who never knew how it felt to stand in the presence of superiors" (LoA, p. 6).

To Whitman, an American, a democratic American, is someone who will never obey the command to kneel. We don't kneel to kings, and we don't kneel to dukes and barons, and we don't kneel to those who are richer or better placed than we are. We don't kneel to God, Jesus, or the saints or Holy Mother church. As Whitman says in the passage on the animals and what they have to show us about our corrupted selves, "Not one kneels to another nor to his kind that lived thousands of years ago" (l. 690). We don't kneel. Period.

But we might also say that to Walt's way of thinking, democratic people do not compel others to kneel either. When a democracy becomes an imperial power and begins dictating its values to others across the world, compelling them to kneel, then it's doing evil.

There are those who say that Whitman lacks a sense of evil: he blesses almost all that surrounds him, and finds everything that lives to be holy. In *Varieties of Religious Experience,* William James calls him a proponent of "the religion of healthy-mindedness." That particular faith does all it can to help banish disagreeable thoughts from the minds of its adherents. James calls Whitman "the supreme contemporary example of [the] inability to feel evil" (p. 82).

There is no truth to this view. Whitman does have a view of evil, simple and profound. Evil for Walt is based on domination. When one person or group stands above another, the result is inevitably evil. When you are compelled to kneel, wrong is being done to you. When you compel others to kneel, you're perpetrating evil. The chief sin in Whitman is abasement—abasement of others and of the self. When one stands above another, cruelty is the inevitable result. Almost every evil in life, Whitman suggests, may lie in the wish to dominate others. He declares it in most memorable terms: "Whoever degrades another degrades me" (l. 504).

Walt, as consistent as he generally is, gets himself into trouble on this score at least once in the poem. Early on in the first major catalogue, he identifies himself glancingly but uncritically with a southern "planter nonchalant and hospitable" (l. 331). To be a southern planter in 1855, you've certainly got to compel others to kneel. Yet overall, Walt stays true to his democratic vision throughout the poem. With his generous imagination, he treats others with kindness and respect and understanding. Is he perfect? No. But if you will only accept truth and revelation from an anointed, blameless angel, you may have a while to wait.

The Mexicans who massacre the rangers are perpetrating evil. The slave catchers who drive the Black man to the ground alongside the fence are doing evil. The men selling the mulatto girl are acting evilly. So too when you abase yourself to another's power and offer no resistance, you are doing ill. ("Obey little, resist much," Walt says.) Those who kneel, and induce their fellows to kneel, to others of their kind who lived thousands of years ago are perpetrating a form of evil. In America, everyone stands, no one kneels—or so it should be.

A SEA FIGHT

The passage about the death of the rangers is perfect Whitman: no one named, no heroes, no one celebrated above anyone else. The bravery here is collective: the men maintain their democratic spirit and will not concede superiority to their victors. No Colonel Travis, no Colonel Bowie, no Davy Crockett, King of the Wild Frontier.

A second tale in Whitman's heroic archive also brings the issue of democratic heroism to the fore. The tale is not an unfamiliar one. It's the story of John Paul Jones and the naval battle between the *Bonhomme Richard* and the *Serapis* during the American Revolution. Jones, the American commander, and his crew withstand a horrible British onslaught and go on to win the engagement. Though the American ship is sinking, the British surrender, and the Americans board their enemy's ship, while their own goes down. It's a thrilling story, and Whitman tells it well.

But the story of "the old fashioned frigate fight" doesn't quite conform to the standards Whitman implicitly sets in the tale of the massacre. Though John Paul Jones is never named in the sequence, he is the center of the action. The plot circulates around him. Whitman, who rather boldly puts himself on the crew of the American ship, refers to Jones as "my little captain" (l. 904). When the British request that the Americans surrender and strike their flag, Whitman's Jones speaks the famous words, "We have not struck, he composedly cried, We have just begun our part of the fighting" (l. 905). Whitman describes the crew, their struggles and suffering: "Near by the corpse of the child that served in the cabin, / The dead face of an old salt with long white hair and carefully curled whiskers" (l. 923).

Yet John Paul Jones, unnamed, is at the center. One moment in particular stands out. Says Whitman:

Serene stood the little captain,
He was not hurried . . . . his voice was neither high nor low,
His eyes gave more light to us than our battle-lanterns. (ll. 914–916)

The captain stands steady, issuing his orders and inspiring courage in his men.

Fine. But note the detail: his eyes give more light than the battle lanterns. It's the sort of trope you might find in Homer: the hero takes on a deific quality. His eyes give off supernatural light. For a moment, the little captain is more than a man. For an instant and maybe more, Whitman has strayed from his implicit vision of democratic heroism.

The question arises: Is it possible to sustain this vision? It's one thing to put a commanding figure at the center of a martial encounter. Maybe that's inevitable. But is it inevitable too to confer superhuman capacities on him, if only for a moment? The scene is surely in some sense feudal. But that only brings forward questions. Is it possible to construct a national vision—a national mythology, if you like—without putting great women and men at the center? Emerson didn't offer the world an *American* mythology per se. Though in *Representative Men* he brought forward Plato, Montaigne, Shakespeare, Goethe, Napoleon, and Swedenborg to create an international canon of the great. Emerson did not want us to be over-awed by greatness, and he tells us so many times. Young men in libraries cower before the images of Locke and Bacon, forgetting that Locke and Bacon were once nothing more than young men in libraries. And that shouldn't be. But the idea of a culture without heroes would have been inadmissible to Emerson.

Maybe a heroless culture is impossible. Freud predicted that America, which he despised, would never amount to much, because its people could not revere extraordinary individuals. Many more writers have stepped forward to tell us, implicitly contra Whitman, that we are hierarchical animals and that we will always create pyramids of domination and submission. We are closer to our ancestors the apes than we realize, they tell us, and similarly obsessed with the powerful among us. And this is all for the good. How far could humanity progress if there were no inducement to lead and create? How far would we go if there were no rewards for extraordinary achievement? The Greeks believed that the best road to immortality is to do deeds that will live forever on the lips of men. If no one cared to speak the name of the hero in the aftertime, there would be nothing to inspire heroes in the present and future, and that would be a major loss. The believer in just fame and hierarchy wants to know why Whitman didn't say the hero's name: John Paul Jones. The radical egalitarian wants to know why Whitman bothered to tell this story at all: the tale of the massacre alone would have been enough. "None obeyed the order to kneel." What more do you need to know?

AMERICAN JESUS

What place does religion have in democracy? When Whitman wrote, America was an overwhelmingly Christian nation, and Christianity remains its predominant faith. Should the citizens of the new democracy continue to worship Jesus? Shall they heed the commandments of the God of the Hebrew Bible? Go to this church or that? Perhaps democratic citizens should drop religion altogether and become atheists, in the mode of Marxist egalitarians.

As *Song of Myself* moves to its close, Whitman begins to take on what might be the most demanding question before him, the religious question. He wants to explore faith and draw conclusions about what Americans of the future might believe. Being Whitman, he doesn't approach the religious question in a conventional way. Wanting to understand what role Jesus ought to have in the democracy, Whitman, flush with the imaginative power he's accrued so far, simply becomes Jesus. And he becomes Jesus in his most perilous hour, the hour of the crucifixion.

Somehow I have been stunned. Stand back!
Give me a little time beyond my cuffed head and slumbers and
    dreams and gaping,
I discover myself on a verge of the usual mistake.

That I could forget the mockers and insults!
That I could forget the trickling tears and the blows of the bludgeons
    and hammers!
That I could look with a separate look on my own crucifixion and
    bloody crowning! (ll. 955–960)

The passage is daring, even for Walt: Whitman becomes the most revered figure in Western culture in an instant, and it would seem, almost casually. "I discover myself on a verge of the usual mistake," says Whitman. What is this usual mistake?

I would speculate that the mistake is believing that Jesus is anything other than a mortal man. If he were more—if he were a god or the son of God—Whitman could not manage to inhabit his body and share his experience. On some level, Jesus is no different from the dying fireman and the hounded slave Walt has imaginatively merged with. Jesus too is within the poet's scope. He's taken a step toward humanizing Jesus, and symbolically dissolving his divinity, as well.

After the death of Jesus, there comes the resurrection, or so the Gospels tell us. Walt might have canceled that part of the story and left us with his conjunction with Jesus in the crucifixion. But he doesn't: in Whitman's rendering, Jesus does rise from the dead. "I resume the overstaid fraction," says Walt, meaning (I think) that there's a bit of business (a fraction) that he's postponed so far. But this construction (if true) is ironic: the business he's conducting now is anything but minor.

> I remember . . . . I resume the overstaid fraction,
> The grave of rock multiplies what has been confided to it . . . . or to
>   any graves,
> The corpses rise . . . . the gashes heal . . . . the fastenings roll away.
>   (ll. 961–963)

Jesus rises from the dead, yes. But so do all the other corpses: all made whole, gashes healed. We all emerge from the tomb with Jesus, but this rising isn't a prelude to ascent into heaven, as it is in the Gospels. Instead it's the beginning of what Walt calls "an average unending procession":

> I troop forth replenished with supreme power, one of an average
>   unending procession,
> We walk the roads of Ohio and Massachusetts and Virginia and
>   Wisconsin and New York and New Orleans and Texas and
>   Montreal and San Francisco and Charleston and Savannah and
>   Mexico,

Inland and by the seacoast and boundary lines . . . . and we pass the
boundary lines. (ll. 964–966)

Walt as Jesus, American Jesus, emerges from the tomb that is the past
to march forward into the future. Jesus is nothing terribly special, nor is
Walt: singly and together they are part of the procession that tramps its
way through the states, "an average unending procession." They have
risen from the sleep of the past into the new world of possibility and walk
forward together into the future, traversing the land. Whitman has transformed the doctrine of Jesus's resurrection. Now it's not about his immortal powers as the son of God. To Walt, the resurrection is an image
for the rebirth of humanity here in the United States of America.

"We pass the boundary lines," says Walt. Literally he means that he
and his compatriots spread their secular faith out into the world. But
boundary-line passing is also a trope for what Whitman is up to overall.
He wants to undo the boundary lines between rich and poor, Black and
White, male and female, educated and unschooled. Conservatism, at its
heart, is about establishing and sustaining the kinds of categories and
boundaries that define and control human life. The true progressive—and
Walt is one—is likely to believe that there are altogether too many bounds
and limitations. The progressive wants to try and test them and, if they
prove needless, wants to erase them—consign them to the past.

Jesus matters because he's the first real democrat. He preaches the
equality of all men and women in the face of the cultures of the Romans
and the Jews. The Jews lived under the authority of the rabbis, the Romans under the authority of the emperor. Both cultures were complexly
structured and hierarchical, though the culture of the rabbis was far
more congenial to Jesus, who draws upon it often. Jesus teaches equality
for all: blessed are the meek, for they shall inherit the earth, and in time,
all of us will be compassionate and mild. This was initially an outrage to
many Jews and to virtually all Romans, among the most competitive and
hierarchical people the world has yet seen. The idea was, at least on first
encounter, almost impossible to comprehend. The people the Romans
went to the coliseum to see butchered weren't human beings at all. They
didn't count. Almost no one who was not a Roman citizen was of consequence. Yet in time, the vision of Jesus overcame the ethos of Rome, and
the seeds for democracy went into the ground.

"Who do men say I am?" says Jesus to his disciples in the Gospel of Mark. Whatever doubts Jesus may or may not have had about his identity, much of the world came in time to regard him as the Son of God. So it was when Whitman lived, so it is today. Whitman writes to de-divinize Jesus. He dissociates Jesus from the Father and from organized religion: there's no mention of God in the crucifixion passage and no mention of heaven. After his resurrection, Walt's Jesus doesn't walk the earth for forty days and forty nights and then ascend into heaven to sit at the right hand of the Father, to come again in glory then to judge the living and the dead. No, Walt makes Jesus a breathing suffering *man,* like me and you, like the slave and the fireman.

The Jesus of the Gospels takes us toward democracy. He constantly preaches the equality of all women and men. Yet his engagement with Yahweh, complex as it may be, still connects him to hierarchical faith—to the Father, to heroes, to feudalism, and to Whitman's spiritual nemesis, the sun. "May this cup pass over," says Jesus to God the Father in the Garden of Gethsemane. "Into thy hands I commend my spirit," he says as he dies on the cross. The Lord God remains at the center of Jesus's overall vision, but Whitman wants a Son who can't be construed as a sun. So he disconnects Jesus from God, and makes him one of the common people. In *Song of Myself,* Jesus is Walt (almost everyone is), and he's also, we might say, the first American.

Walt tries to do to Jesus and his legacy something like what Jesus did to the Hebrew Bible—take it a step forward. Jesus shucks off what he sees as the oppressive laws of the Pharisees, who had rules for every aspect of life. He goes so far as to reduce the Ten Commandments to two: Love the Lord your God with your whole heart, soul, and mind. Second, love your neighbor as yourself. Whitman comes along and reduces the issue further. Now there's only one commandment: Love your neighbor as yourself.

In this late phase of the poem, Whitman puts his religious vision into a set of stories about the development of culture. The only philosopher Whitman ever cared for was Hegel, with his vision of how historical and cultural phases give way to one another. Says Walt in *Democratic Vistas,* "We see that almost everything that has been written, sung, or stated, of old, with reference to humanity under the feudal and oriental institutes, religions, and for other lands, needs to be re-written, re-sung, re-stated, in terms consistent with the institution of these States, and to come in range and obedient uniformity with them" (LoA, p. 993). Whitman understands himself as the spirit of democracy, and he wants to show us how our new order of the world advances beyond other world orders, without obliterating them or violently turning against them.

Now, Whitman and his resurrected fellows are on the march forward into the future:

> Our swift ordinances are on their way over the whole earth,
> The blossoms we wear in our hats are the growth of two thousand
>   years.
>
> Eleves I salute you,
> I see the approach of your numberless gangs . . . . I see you
>   understand yourselves and me,
> And know that they who have eyes are divine, and the blind and
>   lame are equally divine,
> And that my steps drag behind yours yet go before them,
> And are aware how I am with you no more than I am with
>   everybody. (SoM, ll. 967–973)

The blossoms that Whitman and his eleves (his students) wear in their hats are the growth of two thousand years—roughly from the time that Jesus was born to Whitman's present moment. Walt and Jesus are in the eleves' procession, sometimes up front, sometimes in the rear. Says Whitman in the 1855 preface, "The messages of great poets to each man and woman are, Come to us on equal terms, Only then can you understand us, We are no better than you, What we enclose you enclose. What we enjoy you may enjoy. Did you suppose there could be only one Supreme? We affirm there can be unnumbered Supremes, and that one does not countervail another any more than one eyesight countervails another" (LoA, p. 14). Walt is looking forward to the time when throngs will have read *Leaves of Grass* and begun to comprehend his revolutionary message.

DEMOCRATIC GÖTTERDÄMMERUNG

Walt isn't through with established religion yet—he hasn't fully submitted it to his benevolent form of imaginative conquest. He's plucked Jesus out of the history of belief as especially worth saving and even cherishing. But as to other faiths and other figures, Whitman is not quite so welcoming:

> Magnifying and applying come I,
> Outbidding at the start the old cautious hucksters,
> The most they offer for mankind and eternity less than a spirt of my
>   own seminal wet. (SoM, ll. 1020–1022)

The old cautious hucksters? These, as we'll see, include some of the major figures from the religious tradition. And what they offer humanity now—now that democracy has come into the world—is less than a jet of Walt's sperm, which to be sure is capable of creating "landscapes . . . masculine full-sized and golden" (l. 646). Is it necessary to say that no other consequential poet could have written the line about his "seminal wet"? By now, probably not.

Walt's way of dealing with antiquated gods is to collect them all, slap them between bindings, and relegate them to bookshelves where they can rest for eternity. "Houses and rooms are full of perfumes," he told us at the start of the poem: and now Walt's book of the gods can become one among the aromatic irrelevances. The volume will become like most books (if not all) after the coming of democracy and (of course) the coming of *Leaves of Grass*. Then Whitman goes to work transforming the religious past:

Taking myself the exact dimensions of Jehovah and laying them
    away,
Lithographing Kronos and Zeus his son, and Hercules his grandson,
Buying drafts of Osiris and Isis and Belus and Brahma and Adonai,
In my portfolio placing Manito loose, and Allah on a leaf, and the
    crucifix engraved,
With Odin, and the hideous faced Mexitli, and all idols and images,
Honestly taking them all for what they are worth, and not a cent
    more,
Admitting they were alive and did the work of their day,
Admitting they bore mites as for unfledged birds who have now to
    rise and fly and sing for themselves.
Accepting the rough deific sketches to fill out better in myself . . . .
    bestowing them freely on each man and woman I see.
    (ll. 1023–1031)

Jehovah, Zeus, Allah, and the rest: they did some spiritual work in their
time. So did the Egyptian gods Isis and Osiris; Belus, the Babylonian
deity; the Hindu god Brahma; and the war gods Odin (from the Norse
legends) and Mexitli (from the Central American). Adonai? That's a Hebrew name for the Lord God of Hosts. By placing the biblical God in the
list twice, Walt reaffirms his sense that God *as conceived by pious Chris-
tians and Jews* is nothing more than an outmoded entity.

These deities bore tiny pellets of spiritual sustenance to the uncertain,
immature multitudes, who couldn't digest anything stronger. Now it's
time to put them all away because though they offered a prelude to real
spiritual life, we can do better.

Instead of Jehovah and Allah, we have something new. Walt says he
is now:

Discovering as much or more in a framer framing a house,
Putting higher claims for him there with his rolled-up sleeves,
    driving the mallet and chisel;
Not objecting to special revelations . . . . considering a curl of smoke
    or a hair on the back of my hand as curious as any revelation;
Those ahold of fire-engines and hook-and-ladder ropes more to me
    than the gods of the antique wars,

Minding their voices peal through the crash of destruction,
Their brawny limbs passing safe over charred laths . . . . their white
    foreheads whole and unhurt out of the flames;
By the mechanic's wife with her babe at her nipple interceding for
    every person born;
Three scythes at harvest whizzing in a row from three lusty angels
    with shirts bagged out at their waists;
The snag-toothed hostler with red hair redeeming sins past and to
    come,
Selling all he possesses and traveling on foot to fee lawyers for his
    brother and sit by him while he is tried for forgery. (ll. 1032–1041)

I suspect that the framer framing a house is an image of Whitman himself and also of the archetypal carpenter, Jesus of Nazareth, the one figure in the religious tradition who deserves deep respect and affection (but not worship). We don't need celestial angels anymore: the three beautiful harvesters making their scythes sing will do just as well. The mechanic's wife nursing her babe is worth all the reverence in the world, for she embodies the great principle of human thriving and hope, the love of mothers. She replaces the Virgin Mary, the beloved intercessor in Catholic doctrine, for the mechanic's wife is here now and alive now, and her descendants and her contemporaries will all be enriched by her loving kindness. And do we need the tale of the biblical Good Samaritan, when we have an American story about a crooked hosteler redeeming sins past and to come by selling all he has to help out his brother?

If you are looking for instances of beauty and generosity and goodness, you can stop studying old books and look around you to see what Americans are doing now and imagine what they'll do in the future. Democracy releases energies and hopes in people that are worth believing in. Look around and find what Robert Frost in a Whitmanian moment called that which is common in life but rare in books.

Nor should Nature be left out, when we turn to praise and give thanks for what life brings:

What was strewn in the amplest strewing the square rod about me,
    and not filling the square rod then;
The bull and the bug never worshipped half enough,

Dung and dirt more admirable than was dreamed,
The supernatural of no account . . . . myself waiting my time to be
     one of the supremes,
The day getting ready for me when I shall do as much good as the
     best, and be as prodigious,
Guessing when I am it will not tickle me much to receive puffs out
     of pulpit or print;
By my life-lumps! becoming already a creator!
Putting myself here and now to the ambushed womb of the
     shadows! (ll. 1042–1049)

Given all he knows and sees, Whitman tells us that he himself is waiting in line to be like one of the ancient gods. He's joking, naturally. So he is when he projects himself forward in time to the moment when he'll be receiving inflated praise ("puffs") from churches and newspapers—and telling us that it won't phase him much one way or the other. The lines are facetious, at least until he comes to the enigmatic thought about putting himself to the ambushed womb of the shadows. Are his life lumps the bumps on his head that reveal his character? (Walt was a sometime believer in phrenology.) Or are they lumps of his creative sperm—his seminal wet—that sometimes helps bring his poetry into being? The ambushed womb of the shadows? Maybe Walt is referring to some dark and little-explored site of wisdom and vision that he still can visit and in the future will—there to beget more poems. Richard Poirier speculates that the "womb" is ambushed by Whitman's "perennial enemies—critics, other poets, academics, even friendly ones—who threaten to extinguish his chances for a future life among the 'supreme' poets" (p. 284). Maybe so. It is not easy to say. We can say that Walt is full of exuberance at the imaginative victory he believes he's won over the religious tradition—minus Jesus—and he's laughingly going on his way. It feels good to clean the spiritual slate: it feels good to start again.

WALT AND THE PRIESTS

I do not despise you priests," Walt says (l. 1092). But his need to say so indicates that he's at least *tempted*. Still, Whitman is determined to encompass all that he can. He says:

> My faith is the greatest of faiths and the least of faiths,
> Enclosing all worship ancient and modern, and all between ancient and modern,
> Believing I shall come again upon the earth after five thousand years. (ll. 1093–1095)

Like Jesus, Walt will be back, but not coming again in glory, like the Christian Savior, to judge the living and the dead. He'll probably return to check up on the democracy, which by then ought to encompass the globe and maybe pass beyond. Maybe he'll offer a poem or two if the people need to be reminded of their glory. The key word in the passage is "enclosing." Walt has set boundaries around the old religions, as though now they are no more than museum pieces.

Soon Whitman enters into a compressed genealogy of religious practices. He's part of every phase, "waiting responses from oracles," "honoring the gods," and even "saluting the sun." Then forward we go, toward the present:

> Waiting responses from oracles . . . . honoring the gods . . . . saluting the sun,
> Making a fetish of the first rock or stump . . . . powwowing with sticks in the circle of obis,

Helping the lama or brahmin as he trims the lamps of the idols,

Dancing yet through the streets in a phallic procession . . . . rapt and
　　austere in the woods, a gymnosophist,

Drinking mead from the skull-cup . . . . to shastas and vedas
　　admirant . . . . minding the koran,

Walking the teokallis, spotted with gore from the stone and knife—
　　beating the serpent-skinned drum;

Accepting the gospels, accepting him that was crucified, knowing
　　assuredly that he is divine,

To the mass kneeling—to the puritan's prayer rising—sitting
　　patiently in a pew,

Ranting and frothing in my insane crisis—waiting dead-like till my
　　spirit arouses me. (ll. 1096–1104)

This is all a pantomime, of course. Whitman is going through the motions with the priests and devotees down through time. He starts early,
with fetish worship, and moves forward through religious history, more
or less, coming into his present moment with the puritan's prayer and
Catholic mass. He's with the Hindu priests, admiring the *Rig Veda;* he's
devoted to the strictures of the Koran; and he may even be involved in
human sacrifice in a Mesoamerican temple wielding a bloody knife.

Whitman generally uses his lists to celebrate people and natural wonders. He especially delights in using them to put all humans on the same
level: the president and the slave girl come in sequence. By putting the
Christian mass and puritan prayer in the same list as tree fetishism and
human sacrifice, he cuts them down to size. As to accepting the divinity
of Jesus, Walt can imagine doing so, and imagine others doing so. But
all that is in the past.

Perhaps the most resistant identity for Whitman to enter into is the
atheist's:

Down-hearted doubters, dull and excluded,

Frivolous sullen moping angry affected disheartened atheistical,

I know every one of you, and know the unspoken interrogatories,

By experience I know them. (ll. 1109–1112)

The atheists are the worst by far, but Whitman can embrace them too.
It's not easy, not at all. This may be in part because, as Walt suggests, he's

been one of them. "By experience," he says, "I know them." The line harks back to the beginning of the poem, when Walt is mapping the limitations of the worldly Self. "Backward I see in my own days where I sweated through fog with linguists and contenders" (l. 71). No more empty word games for Walt: religion is too important for that. Now that he has discovered and developed his Soul, he can say good-bye to sterile argument.

Walt may never have had to reach so far and with so much effort as he does to embrace the atheists. But he can at last say, "Be at peace bloody flukes of doubters and sullen mopers, / I take my place among you as much as among any" (ll. 1115–1116). Flukes? Flukes are the tails on leviathan, the whale, and also the barbs on the harpoons that whalers use to kill them. Does Whitman see the doubters as a school of wounded, bleeding fish, lost and maybe doomed? I'm not sure. The line doesn't seem fully cogent. Yet Walt is a little like Emily Dickinson, some of whose poems have seemed incoherent, even nonsensical—until a devoted reader finally comes along to find persuasive meaning. Her powers of mind are larger than ours, and yes, she's usually making more sense than we previously imagined. So it is with Walt.

Atheism is a dreadful error: it's sterile and life-denying. Its proponents lack gratitude and affection. Other forms of worship have their appeal, even if it's a bizarre appeal. But they are not Walt's forms at all. What, then, is the correct answer to the question of God? How shall we believe? In whom? For what purpose? Is there a God who transcends democracy?

WALT'S GOD

Walt has no committed interest in organized religion: he'll encompass its ways; he'll even take on the priestly role, playfully for the most part, in imagination; but he's not going to succumb to established faith. Nor is he going to embrace atheism. He's not going to turn himself into a commonplace unbeliever, obsessed with proving to the world once and for all that God does not exist and can't. Atheists are the sort of people Whitman vied with before he really began his shamanistic voyage. But they mean nothing to him now. He treats them more disdainfully than he does the priests.

But God, what about God? On the matter of God, Whitman can seem quite aggressive.

> I have said that the soul is not more than the body,
> And I have said that the body is not more than the soul,
> And nothing, not God, is greater to one than one's self is.
>   (SoM, ll. 1262–1264)

You can read this a couple of ways, if you like. It can say that the self is greater than God; it can also say that nothing that is not God is greater than the self but that God actually is. It's probably the former, but even then, there is some subtlety involved. If you are thinking the right way, we'll see, you simply aren't thinking all that much about God. So you should matter more than the deity because the deity, as Whitman goes on to tell us, is both a miraculous force and a source of profound unconcern.

Let it go, says Whitman. Give up the fixation on God and proceed with your proper business, which is to sustain and enjoy life righteously:

> And I call to all mankind, Be not curious about God,
> For I who am curious about each am not curious about God,
> No array of terms can say how much I am at peace about God and
>   about death. (ll. 1271–1273)

Whitman is not saying that there is no God. It's simply that we democratic Americans have no reason to spend our lives brooding on his essence, which is not going to disclose itself to us anyway.

Whitman is working his way toward his ultimate statement about God, which is as profound as it is simple and seemingly off-hand: "I hear and behold God in every object, yet I understand God not in the least" (l. 1274). This is an amazing line: the world is stunning; creation is a joy and sometimes a terror. "A mouse," as Whitman has told us, "is miracle enough to stagger sextillions of infidels" (l. 668). All that lives is holy. All that breaths, divine. Love it. Worship it if you like. But there is no need to return to its ultimate cause and prostrate yourself. Give thanks for existence, even if there is no one to thank. Stop trying to figure out what God wants you to do and figure out what you want to do and what democracy needs you to do. Democracy is the true God at least on this earth. You don't have to worship it; just jump in and make it happen.

God is in our wonder at the existence of the world. We experience God when we stand in awe and gratitude at what is before us. Jesus is a democratic man, like you and me and Walt; God is the life that gives life and beyond that is nothing but joyous mystery. There's no reason to go around shouting about God or trying to worship or know or placate him. Shut up and enjoy what he brings. Here are Whitman's great lines, designed to help us and our fellow Americans get their eyes out of the clouds and love what is before us:

> Why should I wish to see God better than this day?
> I see something of God each hour of the twenty-four, and each
>   moment then,
> In the faces of men and women I see God, and in my own face in the
>   glass;

> I find letters from God dropped in the street, and every one is signed
>   by God's name,
> And I leave them where they are, for I know that others will
>   punctually come forever and ever. (ll. 1276–1280)

If there are truer words about God, I do not know quite where to find them—or at least truer words to fit the new world that Whitman is hoping to help create.

The letters from God are like the manna God dropped from heaven for the Israelites while they wandered in the desert. The Jews were instructed to take only what they needed for a day and leave the rest. When they took more, the manna stopped coming. Just so, signs of God are all around us. Accept them with gratitude and grace. But your time is not going to be well spent investigating every one of them to learn, finally, the nature of God. If you do start to inquire into God's letters, you may become obsessed by them and stop seeing the divinity that exists in every object. The manna will stop coming. God is an amazement. But admit that, enjoy it, then get about the business of having a democratic good time in this world.

Richard Rorty's reflections on Whitman and God are illuminating: "Whitman thought that we Americans have the most poetical nature because we are the first thoroughgoing experiment in national self-creation: the first nation-state with nobody but itself to please—not even God. We are the greatest poem because we put ourselves in the place of God: our essence is our existence, and our existence is in the future. Other nations thought of themselves as hymns to the glory of God. We redefine God as our future selves" (p. 22). Our God, Rorty argues, is what we hope to become over time: a better, more encompassing country. We don't have a finite, immediate nature that's readily defined. Rather, we are our actions as we unfold them into the future. We do not have an essential being; we are all about becoming.

Oh, yes—and don't worry too much about dying. As Walt says, "No array of terms can say how much I am at peace about God and about death" (l. 1273).

Really? How can that be so?

WALT AND THE READER

Whitman has come a long way on his quest. He has every right to be weary, every right to be proud. He's put the literature of the past in its place, gone outside to become undisguised and naked; and, in the guise of the Self, he's beckoned his Soul forward, then joined Self and Soul in his wonderfully outrageous love scene. From there he overcomes inertia—Walt hates standing still—and he's on the move. He can see God and feel his presence, and he can also sound the bass note of creation: touching the elder, mullen, and pokeweed and the scabs beneath the wormfence. His imagination yields more rewards to him: he's now in a position to create his master trope for democracy, simple as it is profound: the grass. Then he's off, afoot with his visions.

Whitman sees the democracy from high above and celebrates the work, the suffering, and the joy that comes with being an American. He savors not only his fellow citizens but also nature, the miraculous expanse of territory that is our home. He's also in love with "these states"—small nations in themselves that are still part of the glorious larger whole. And he conveys his love for the states to us in memorable words.

Walt soon arrives at his counterimage to the grass, the sun. The sun is alone, overpowering, authoritative, and would do away with Walt if he, like all of us, couldn't "now and always send sunrise out of" himself (l. 563). The sun is old King Sol. And though he's had his day at the regal center, times are shifting. Then comes that all-important if enigmatic autoerotic scene at the center of the poem—and matters darken. Whitman broods on the animals and violence and the kind of courage that fits a democracy. There's the encounter with religion—with Walt writing his American-Hegelian genealogies and rescuing Jesus for future use. Finally, of course, he considers God—in whom Walt is surely a believer, albeit after his own fashion.

What about Walt himself? Who exactly is he? Is he one of us—a member of the democracy, a simple blade of grass? Or is he a new prophet so profoundly inspired that he might demand our worship, one of "the Supremes"? Having questioned the old sun, is Walt anything more than an aspiring new one? This question matters for our understanding of the poem but also for our vision of distinction in a democracy. Are there to be no great ones to inspire us on? Must all be leveled to the same ground?

In an extended section of the poem, Walt offers an answer to the question of his own identity and of his relations to us, his readers. Actually, he offers multiple answers. Perhaps too many. Here's the first, in which Walt looks ahead to the day when the reader will wander on without him:

> Sit awhile wayfarer,
> Here are biscuits to eat and here is milk to drink,
> But as soon as you sleep and renew yourself in sweet clothes I will
>   certainly kiss you with my goodbye kiss and open the gate for
>   your egress hence.
>
> Long enough have you dreamed contemptible dreams,
> Now I wash the gum from your eyes,
> You must habit yourself to the dazzle of the light and of every
>   moment of your life. (ll. 1222–1227)

Now there is another answer, far more dramatic and even aggressive. One is most surprised to hear so agonistic a farewell from Walt:

> I am the teacher of athletes,
> He that by me spreads a wider breast than my own proves the width
>   of my own,
> He most honors my style who learns under it to destroy the teacher.
>   (ll. 1231–1233)

Then there is a third, mild and sweet but asserting that Walt will be with us, his readers, always, for who having once encountered him can ever escape his influence?

> I teach straying from me, yet who can stray from me?
> I follow you whoever you are from the present hour;
> My words itch at your ears till you understand them.

> I do not say these things for a dollar, or to fill up the time while I
>   wait for a boat;
> It is you talking just as much as myself . . . . I act as the tongue of you,
> It was tied in your mouth . . . . in mine it begins to be loosened.
>   (ll. 1240–1245)

Walt is many things in these passages. He's the benevolent guide who gives us food and drink and then sends us off on our way, beyond him and into our lives. But he's also the agonistic instructor who, sounding much like Emerson and even more like Nietzsche, tells us how the best of students are the ones who "destroy" their teachers. (The line may be the most un-Whitmanian in the poem, asserting that struggle, rather than benevolent assimilation, is the best way to deal with troubling influences.) In the third farewell, we're to stray from Walt—but then, who can stray from Walt? In this passage, we don't overcome the poet, and we don't strike out without him; here he lives within us, for once we've met him, there is no going back.

It's clear that Walt doesn't really know how he wants us to take him. Surely he's alert to the dangers of becoming another pseudomonarch. He's not willing to affirm himself out and out as an Emersonian master. But exactly who is he in relation to his reader?

It's possible, I think, that Walt has already done some of the work of establishing who and what he is. In the autoerotic scene, Walt opened himself up to us as bravely as any writer has. He's been willing to reveal himself, willing to risk humiliation. No one who is so open about his idiosyncratic desires could ever be a king or a potentate. The king embodies an image of perfection—his narcissism is perfect, he loves only himself, and he never betrays anything about his own being that could serve to demystify him. Walt is self-exalting throughout the poem—though he would say that he is exalting each and all of us too. We have our bodies, as he has his. We have nature. We can live joyfully in the world. But at the center of the poem, he sends forth an image of himself that is completely incompatible with the role of the leader, maximum authority, or, as Lacan usefully puts it, subject who is *supposed* to know it all, *le sujet supposé savoir*. With his candor, Whitman begins to deconstruct whatever aspirations he may have to being a king or potentate.

Still, for many readers, this might not resolve the issue of authority. It's not at all uncommon, even among sympathetic readers of the poem, to criticize Walt as an imperialist of the imagination. How dare he speak for me? How dare he speak for everyone? How can he possibly speak for women and people of color?

Those who pose these questions often have what seems to me an exaggerated sense of authority overall and of literary authority in particular. Yes, Walt does want to be the voice of democracy and everyone in it, however hard that might be to achieve. But his authority isn't the authority of the totalitarian leader, whose words the citizen is compelled to echo, on pain of imprisonment or death. The dictator, as the name implies, is the nonstop talker, whose words we had better take as bindingly true.

I think it's best to see Walt, and virtually every other imaginative writer of consequence, as issuing not edicts but *invitations*. Walt asks us to make his words ours, his vision our own. Though he can be declarative, no one could possibly call him coercive. What happens if you simply walk away from him, and return to the existing complex of beliefs and values you possess? What if having read the poem, you return to the words and thoughts that Rorty would call your own "final vocabulary," uninfluenced by Walt? What happens is absolutely nothing. You read Whitman and didn't care for him, *tant pis*.

Or you can respond more actively. You can write your own poems: they can be a rebuttal to Walt, inspired by Walt, or both at once. You will not be the first to write under Whitman's influence, far from it. Pound disliked Whitman but claimed to have made a poetic pact with him. Lawrence, Lorca, Neruda, Borges, Pessoa, Paz, Vallejo, and Langston Hughes have all taken inspiration from Whitman. So too have Hart Crane, Willa Cather, Adrienne Rich, June Jordan, Maxine Hong Kingston, and Bob Dylan.

Still, the issue of authority can linger for some readers. I think that Walt completes *Song of Myself* after the poem is over. Though in the autoerotic scene he's offered a self-demystification that contributes to his standing as no more than one of us, an American everyday person, there's further to go. In the Washington, DC, hospitals, during the Civil War, he'll answer the question of greatness, his and others', not with words but with deeds.

DEATH AND DEMOCRACY

Walt tells us that death does not concern him much. "No array of terms can say how much I am at peace about God and about death." Really? Are we to believe him? As his students (his "eleves"), we might like to earn the same attitude. For how fine it would be to be at peace about death!

In fact, being at peace about death may be a prerequisite for getting all that Walt says there is to get out of democracy. For what democracy can offer us is presence, unity, and individuality: presence within the moment, unity with our fellow democrats, and the chance to be ourselves day to day. The way into the "average unending procession" is through the achievement of presence and unity and singularity of self.

Presence: that means not always being yoked to the past or achingly looking toward the future, where death abides. Unity: that is the feeling of belonging in the world and not being an outcast. Even if you are an orphan, you'll never be outcast in a real democracy. You are also singular: though your collective being matters most, you are you, and there never was and never will be another grass blade of quite the same contours and the same shade of green. If you can overcome the problem of death, you can look to achieving unity and presence and singularity of self.

Whitman talks a lot about death, but his most important statement may come down to a few lines. It is simple: he is ending the poem, and he is taking his leave of us, his readers, after performing his miracle. He is ending his poem, and he is also reflecting on the ending of his life in the world. Here are his lines of farewell:

I depart as air . . . . I shake my white locks at the runaway sun,
I effuse my flesh in eddies and drift it in lacy jags.

I bequeath myself to the dirt to grow from the grass I love,
If you want me again look for me under your bootsoles.

You will hardly know who I am or what I mean,
But I shall be good health to you nevertheless,
And filter and fibre your blood.

Failing to fetch me at first keep encouraged,
Missing me one place search another,
I stop some where waiting for you (ll. 1327–1336)

"I bequeath myself to the dirt to grow from the grass I love," Walt says, an infinitely suggestive line.

The concluding passage can give us some hints about how democratic people square themselves with death. But let's think first about how aristocratic people do. To the Romans, who created the most aristocratic of cultures, there are a few ways to live beyond your span on earth. The first is through doing great deeds. Julius Caesar will live forever; so will Augustus; so Pompey the Great. They'll be part of the noble history of the Roman people. Then, not as desirable but not without value, one may live on through one's words. Public words are probably best, oratory. Cicero will not die, but the works of the poets matter too: Virgil first among all, but surely Horace and Martial as well. One is ranked: the best of the soldiers and emperors lives longest on the tongues of men; the best orators, the most quoted and admired poets live on too. If you have neither martial deeds nor memorable words to recommend you, you can live on through your descendants: to the Romans, family is of maximum importance. You are your clan. But to live on only because your family continues through time is a pale achievement compared to the works of eloquent speakers and conquering generals.

Through deeds, through glowing words, through founding or supplying a distinguished line, you live into the future. As a Roman, your life has been agonistic. You struggled against other races, nations, empires for the glory of Rome. You also struggled against your Roman contemporaries. Who is the best soldier? The second? Whose words will ring out when Rome finally collapses into the Tiber? Riding through a mud-caked village in Gaul, Julius Caesar remarked to his companion that he would prefer to be the first man there amid the dirt and squalor than the second man in Rome. Competition is everywhere in the classical world, the precursor of the feudal sphere. Achievement gives you standing in this life and a measured immortality. And perhaps this takes some of the sting out of death.

But Whitman has another answer to the problem of death. At the end of his poem, Whitman wants to be reincarnated, not as president or mogul or chieftain but as grass, grass that we can look down at and see beneath our shoes. And this is what we all should consider wanting—not immortality through words or deeds or distinguished descendants but ongoing life as grass blades.

We're all going to die in the body and become compost. We're going to feed the earth, feed the grass. Unless you truly love nature, *truly* love it, that's not going to do much for you. But think of the figurative dimension. If you live as a blade of grass, among other blades, your passing into brown from vibrant green will feed the existing expanse of grass that is democracy. If you've managed to live a democratic life, you'll have done something to contribute to the ongoing venture that is the free and equal society. And in that future democratic nation, you'll be kept alive. You will achieve immortality because democracy does. In your daily life, you will be making a future for the greatest idea about how to live and govern (and to love) that humanity has ever had.

Your contribution matters. It matters because democracy's success is not guaranteed: it may fade and die. After Athens and a few other Greek city-states dissolved, democracy disappeared from the world for what amounted to two thousand years. There were intimations from the Vikings (maybe), intimations from the Seven Nations (perhaps). But for about two millennia, there simply was nothing like committed democracy. There was no real reason that it would be reborn again. (But it was.) There is no real reason that it will last. (But maybe it will.) Whitman understood what a gamble the whole enterprise was. He saw that the odds against were real. He realized and taught us to imagine that if you do all you can for democracy, when you are about to die, you will be able to look back on the work you've put in and the laughter you've laughed in something like the same way that composers look back on their symphonies or painters on their paintings. You'll see that you lived for something. Your life had a meaning.

Just so, while you are alive, you may (just may) be able to worry about death a little less because you are contributing to something that will out-last you. Your life (your blade of grass) will go to fertilize and strengthen the lives of future generations of Americans who know enough to walk away from the perfumes, find Self, find Soul, not be worried about being just one grass blade, and watch out for the sun.

What Walt seems to suggest is that if you immerse yourself fully in the democracy—become that grass blade—you will achieve a certain kind of immortality. The way of life that you have committed yourself to will go on, even after you've departed. You've contributed to some-thing great: so you can pass peacefully from the world believing that it will continue. You are in a sense—but only in a sense—immortal.

This is a lot to ask anyone to embrace. It is not easy to imagine losing one's fear of death because you can believe that the greatest human project of all time will go on after you. But perhaps one can imagine people evolving to the point where they might. Some readers think of Whitman as a poet of reassuring platitudes. He is actually a demanding poet, not only in what he asks of us as readers and interpreters but in what he asks of us humanly. One wonders sometimes, Could we ever become Walt Whitman's contemporaries? One wonders, Could even Whitman ever embody his vision outside the poem—bring it to life?

At the end of the poem, Walt affirms the grass that he loves and takes a glance back at his old foe:

> I depart as air . . . . I shake my white locks at the runaway sun,
> I effuse my flesh in eddies and drift it in lacy jags.
>
> I bequeath myself to the dirt to grow from the grass I love,
> If you want me again look for me under your bootsoles.
>   (ll. 1327–1330)

Walt affirms the grass, and he also declares victory, casually enough: "I shake my white locks at the runaway sun." The sun is running scared from Walt's *Song*—and it should! He's rightfully pushed it aside. After reading Walt's poem, you can look into the sky and see the sun as a simple, grand natural phenomenon and not the emblem for power it's been in the past. The sun will be back, always, reasserting itself. But Walt's there too, in the grass beneath our feet.

The final line of *Song* doesn't conclude with a period: it's open-ended, waiting for us to join in, maybe, and complete it for ourselves after our own fashion. Walt also goes on to complete *Song,* and in a surprising way. He continues to develop his vision after 1855. And though he writes some splendid poems, I think that the real completion to *Song of Myself* does not come through words but through deeds. During the Civil War, as a hospital visitor in Washington, DC, Walt brings his vision out into life to save himself and to inspire all who care to see. He becomes a version of the democratic individual that he prophesies in his poem.

PART II

In the Hospitals

PUBLICATION

Whitman did all he could to advance the fortunes of the 1855 *Leaves of Grass*. He reviewed the book himself, not once but three times. "An American Bard at last," he crowed. Whitman, the New Yorker, was commercially minded. Quickly, he got to work on a new edition. He wrote more poems and published them a year later in the edition of 1856. This volume is short and squat, a quarto, not an expansive folio like the 1855. It looks to be loaded with compact muscle.

Whitman did something memorable to the 1856 volume, which he published himself, something that Emerson probably never fully forgave him for. He took a line from the moving letter that Emerson sent him to celebrate the first edition of *Leaves* and embossed it in gold on the spine of the book. "I greet you at the beginning of a great career, R. W. Emerson," the binding says. Whitman neglected to ask Emerson's permission, and, we're told, the Sage of Concord was quite angry with the American Bard. Emerson did regain his equanimity—in which he put considerable stock—though this was not the last time that he would grow unhappy with the pupil who turned out to be more than a pupil. In the new book, Whitman included a long letter to Emerson, in which he addressed him as "master." Perhaps that helped calm the sage down.

The 1856 volume didn't do what Whitman hoped—none of his volumes really did. He wanted his books to pass into the hands of "the people." He wanted the people he celebrated to read and enjoy the celebration. That didn't happen in 1855 or 1856 or in 1860, when the third volume of *Leaves* came out. At the end of his life, at the close of a birthday celebration in Camden, New Jersey, that moved Whitman to tears, he still mourned the fact that his work had never really reached what he thought of as his true audience. Maybe this is so because Whitman presents in-surmountable *conceptual* and *metaphorical* difficulties. Perhaps it's also that his vision, though cogent and reasonably consistent, remains far out ahead of us. All through his life, Whitman kept trying.

Whitman published other notable poems in the 1855 edition, especially the ones that would be titled "There Was a Child Went Forth," "The Sleepers," and "Boston Ballad." After 1855 came the strange and moving elegy "When Lilacs Last in the Dooryard Bloom'd," as well as "Crossing Brooklyn Ferry," "Out of the Cradle Endlessly Rocking," and "As I Ebb'd with the Ocean of Life." Whitman also composed some wonderful short poems, such as "I Saw in Louisiana a Live-Oak Growing," "When I Heard the Learn'd Astronomer," and "A Noiseless Patient Spider." Virtually all of Whitman's poems have at least one or two memorable lines. Yet much of his work after 1855, and almost all of it after 1865, has something of a programmatic air. It's as though Whitman is writing commentary on *Song of Myself.* He had experienced an astonishing vision. But what ex-actly did the vision mean? What were its implications? And maybe most important, how might he and his country live it out?

Not long after the 1856 edition came out, Whitman moved back to Brooklyn with his mother and extended family, to live in a basement apartment. The family had to rent out the top floor to keep itself even marginally solvent. Whitman wrote poems and some journalistic pieces for a few dollars here and there. He still composed constantly. Walt turned almost every consequential experience into words. But gradually his studied and happy indolence turned into aimlessness: loafing became lassitude. His interest in writing poems dwindled.

Almost every day, Whitman traveled from Brooklyn, usually by ferry, to Manhattan. There he spent his time at a below-ground Broadway es-tablishment called Pfaff's. The restaurant was the meeting place for a group of American artists, actors, journalists, actresses, and writers, who thought of themselves as Bohemians. The man who brought the Bohe-mian life over from Paris was a Nantucket born and raised writer and editor named Henry Clapp. Clapp had been to Paris, where he'd lived for a couple of years on the Left Bank, acquiring a French mistress and learning to live the sensuous, lazy life of French cafes and theater. Clapp was the main figure at the long table under Broadway, where the Bohe-mians gathered.

Pfaff, the proprietor, was German, rotund, gregarious, and hospitable. He seems to have loved filling his restaurant with the fast and slightly scandalous figures who came to sit with Clapp, shoot the breeze, indulge in duels of wit, and plan great futures for themselves. Among the wits, Clapp was preeminent. Of his rival editor Horace Greeley (my ancestor, I was told as a boy), Clapp said, he's a "self-made man who worships his creator." Women as well as men sat at the long table: among them Ada Clare, the "Queen of Bohemia," and Adah Menken, the most notorious actress of the day, who rode onto the stage wearing a nude body stocking in a play based on Byron's *Beppo.* Whitman sat at the long table too—though there was little of the wit about him. He was prone to quiet conversation with the Bohemians sitting closest, but more than that, he was inclined to listen. Whitman was as devoted a listener as he was an observer. Everyone who knew him at Pfaff's seems to have liked him.

The primary Bohemian, Clapp was an early champion of Whitman's work, and never ceased in his admiration for the poet or his willingness to help publicize him. Whitman drank at Pfaff's, but not very much. It seems a beer would last him through the night. He occasionally had a glass of champagne. His abstemious ways and relative silence didn't stop him from becoming a figure there. He was known as the author of a scandalous volume—the erotic side of Whitman's poetry had been excoriated in a dozen ways by at least a dozen reviewers. He also dressed the part of the avant-garde artist: slouch hat, open shirt, pants tucked into high boots. His beard had gone richly a-flower. He looked like someone to reckon with, which in his way he was.

But Whitman didn't spend all his time at Pfaff's sitting at the long table and listening to the wits vie with each other for Clapp's approval. There was another table closer to the center of the tavern that Whitman also favored. This one was populated by young men, whose company Whitman apparently relished as much as he did that of the wits. Was it what we would call a gay culture that Whitman was involved in? It's not certain.

For some time, Whitman had been drawn to the company of males, usually young and working class. He listed their names in his journals, walked with them, talked with them, hugged and kissed them, and occasionally slept with them. Was there sex involved? None of Whitman's behavior was unusual for midcentury America, where intense same-sex friendships arose between men and women alike. Many women approached Whitman with romance in mind. He fended them off, usually with some charm. But he pursued intimate relations with men quite frequently. Were they ever consummated? Of Whitman's prominent critics, Richard Poirier seems most certain that Whitman led a thriving sexual life during his Broadway days. David Reynolds, the author of a comprehensive volume on Whitman and his cultural milieu, is far less certain. On the matter of Whitman and homosexual sex, he's an agnostic, as am I.

Many of the men Whitman befriended during his days at Pfaff's were stage drivers. They drove horse-drawn wagons ferrying passengers and freight up and down Broadway. Broadway could be chaotic: few traffic regulations, little enforcement of those that existed, busy people hustling in all directions. Accidents were common, fights between the drivers frequent. Many of the drivers got hurt, some of them badly. Whitman, who often rode up on the box with them as they banged their ways up and down Broadway, was a loyal friend. When they were injured, he visited them in the hospital. He sat by their bedsides, talked with them, joked, offered them tobacco and other small gifts. He also did one of the things he did best: he listened. Whitman could sit by the hour at a driver's bed, learning about who he was, where he came from, what his dreams were, and where his problems lay. The drivers liked and respected Whitman, and in the hospital, his connections with them strengthened.

There was sometimes a forced, nearly hysterical quality about the revelry at Pfaff's during the late 1850s. America was moving closer to war. Many of the regulars pretended to ignore the coming cataclysm, but not Whitman. He worried for his nation. He had appointed himself its personal bard, and he believed that the welfare of any nation, but especially a democracy, was much in the hands of its poets. Whitman was furiously committed to the idea of Union. The United States must stay one and whole. If it did not, the democratic ideal might go down as a failure. Whitman did all he could in his poems and journalism to fight for national unity. In this, he was much like Lincoln: Whitman detested slavery, but the prospect of disunion was his principal anxiety. Lincoln said that if he could save the Union without freeing a single slave, he would do so. Whitman the citizen and journalist would have concurred: though as we've seen, Whitman the visionary nurtured other aspirations about race in democratic America.

America was moving toward crisis, and the denizens of Pfaff's, Whitman included, were dealing with it in their various ways. Whitman wrote and brooded, brooded and wrote, and braced himself for the moment when his beloved Union would undergo major challenge. Walt saw Lincoln for the first time on Tuesday, February 19, 1861, when the president went to New York, on the way to Washington, DC, for his inauguration. Whitman was one of a crowd of thirty thousand gathered on Broadway to get a look at the president-elect. Walt saw Lincoln leave his carriage, mount the steps of the Astor Hotel, turn, take a slow, melancholy look around, then disappear behind closed doors. Lincoln did not speak a word to the crowds that had gathered to see him. (Or so Whitman says—others claim he made brief remarks.) Whitman was on the top of a stagecoach when he saw Lincoln, the man who would fascinate and move him for the next four years and beyond. Looking back, Whitman recalled how "two or three shabby hack barouches [four-wheeled horse-drawn carriages] made their way with some difficulty through the crowd, and drew up at the Astor House entrance. A tall figure step'd out of the centre of these barouches, paus'd leisurely on the sidewalk, look'd up at the granite walls and looming architecture of the grand old hotel—then after a relieving stretch of arms and legs, turn'd round for over a minute to slowly and good-humoredly scan the appearance of the vast and silent crowds" (LoA, p. 1038).

A handful of states had already left the Union by the day that Whitman saw Lincoln arrive in New York, and before long, Southern troops fired on Fort Sumter. War was on. The next two years were among the worst of Walt's life. He was too old to fight: he was now in his forties, and all the beefsteak, champagne, and butter he'd consumed at Pfaff's had made him portly. Whitman had been terrified by the idea of Civil War—he hated the thought of the states being at deadly odds with each other. (The states being in tension with one another was fine with Walt: he wanted as much diversity and even opposition as possible, without fracture.) Once war came, Whitman became a fierce proponent of Northern victory. Lincoln called for mass enlistment, and Whitman wrote a poem—not one of his best—seconding the call. Whitman continued to write poetry and some journalism from the start of the war through to 1862, but these were among his worst days.

He simply did not know what to do with himself. What should the bard of America do when his nation was split and its citizens were off trying to kill one another? Whitman rambled and wrote a little, wrote some and rambled. But he was living with no sense of purpose. The casualty reports rolled in, and what had seemed like it would be a short war went on and on. The new recruits who marched out of New York City to fight the Rebs left with ropes tied around the barrels of their rifles, each planning to drag a Confederate recruit back home with him. Matters didn't go as planned. The soldiers who enlisted on the Union side generally couldn't imagine the war would last four months—it would continue for four years. Whitman, lost in a purgatory of his own, had no sense what to do.

Then one day, everything changed. George Whitman, Walt's younger brother, had enlisted at Lincoln's first call for volunteers. He was one of the men who'd gone off with a rope around his rifle. George was an anomaly in the Whitman family: sane, affectionate, decent, unimaginative, and practical. Walt loved him deeply, as he loved all his family, and was perpetually anxious about George's fate. After every major battle George fought in, and there were plenty of them, the Whitman family searched through the casualty reports for his name. George emerged from one engagement after another unharmed.

Then came the Battle of Fredericksburg, which left thirteen thousand Union soldiers dead or wounded in a single day. The Whitmans knew that George was deployed near the battle site and began searching the newspapers for word of him. The *New York Tribune* carried news of a First Lieutenant George Whitmore of the Fifty-First New York, George's regiment, who'd been wounded. How badly, the paper didn't say. Surely this could be a transcription or a printing error, the Whitmans thought: this could be their George. Almost immediately, Walt was off to find his brother and make sure he was all right.

Whitman was a resourceful traveler, and in only a few days, he made it to the front lines, found George's regiment, and then, in short order, George. George was fine. A piece of shrapnel had sliced into his cheek, but he was well and in his usual high spirits. (How George emerged from the Whitman family as healthy, hearty, and relatively commonplace as he was is no small mystery.) Whitman was fascinated by life in the camp, and quickly made friends with the soldiers. (Whitman, true to the persona of *Song,* was about as gregarious and friendly as it was possible for an inwardly attuned individual to be.) He ate with the soldiers, sharing their rations; he learned about the battles they'd fought and about their backgrounds and their aspirations for life after the war. He liked them a great deal—no surprise, Whitman cherished the company of everyday young American men—and apparently the soldiers took quickly to Walt. George was already well regarded in the regiment: he was reliable, brave, and good-humored. Walt's spirits, depressed for months, began to rise.

On the first day at camp, Walt saw something that shocked and fascinated him. An engagement was recently over, and there outside the surgical tent, he saw a hill of amputated arms and legs. The surgeons were still at work, and Walt, not terribly squeamish, no stander above men and women in their distress, went into the field hospital and even into the surgeons' tent and watched and wondered. He gave what help he could—Whitman wasn't a trained nurse, but he assisted with basic tasks, like moving the wounded soldiers from place to place. When he could, he sat with the wounded men and talked with them and joked and—compassionate (and authentically modest) bard that he was—he listened. He did for the soldiers much of what he'd done for the Broadway stage drivers when they were hurt. Not far away the formidable nurse Clara Barton was working headlong to help the fallen. Whitman watched Barton in amazement, and understood he could never do what she with her nurse's training could. But slowly an idea seemed to gather in him.

He was feeling alive for the first time in months. It wasn't enough to write poems about the war; it wasn't enough to write journalistic pieces, though Whitman wrote some effective dispatches from the camps. He wanted to do more, and now he saw what, given his talents and his heart's inclination, he might contribute.

IN WASHINGTON

S oon Walt was in Washington, DC, attending on what he called "the great army of the sick." It's now that Whitman becomes more than the poet of *Song of Myself* and begins to become a manifestation of his poetic vision.

To complete the work of *Song*, Whitman left the everyday world and entered into a hellish zone. Everywhere around him were men in torment: soldiers wounded, sick, and dying. They had been brought by trainloads and boatloads from the battlefields of Virginia to the capital of the Union to be cared for, as well as resources and the state of medical knowledge allowed. Some would recover and rejoin their regiments. Some would go home, often without an arm or a leg or as victims of double amputation.

Many would die there in Washington. They died away from their friends in the regiment, away from their friends at home, separated by miles from their families, who often did not know where they were. Many of them died alone—and a number more would have if they had not been visited and attended to by a shambling, kindly old man (to the men, Walt in his forties seemed old), who was also the greatest poet that America has ever produced.

As Roy Morris Jr., the author of *The Better Angel,* a beautiful and perceptive book about Whitman's life during the Civil War, puts it:

> At the time of Whitman's arrival in the capital . . . those who languished in the whitewashed wooden sheds, converted government buildings, and outlying tent hospitals were, practically speaking, the sickest and most gravely wounded of all. By the time they had made

their way to Washington, the soldiers had already endured the disease-ridden squalor of camp life, the exhaustions of marching, the terrors of combat, the chills of fever, the hammering of bullets, the slicing of cannister, and the dull grinding rasp of the surgeon's saw. In many ways their greatest trials still lay ahead. Before they could return to their regiments or, better yet, walk through the gates of their peacetime homes, honorably discharged from the army with an empty sleeve or a brace of crutches, they first had to survive the hospitals. (p. 89)

The men whom Whitman began to visit in Washington were not only wounded but sick, many of them wasting away from chronic illnesses. Diarrhea struck half of the Union troops and almost all the Confederates, eventually killing over a hundred thousand soldiers. They died protracted, humiliating deaths. Whitman was there to comfort as many of them as he could.

In the final days of 1862, when Whitman came to Washington, there were about thirty-five hospitals in and around the capital, with about thirteen thousand soldiers being treated (Morris, pp. 88–89). The conditions were astonishingly bad. Doctors had no idea that diseases were transported by germs, so no one took care to keep the facilities particularly clean. One of the hospitals was located on a site that had been used to quarter horses: the germs from their manure quickly permeated the place, and men grew sick and died from them (Morris, pp. 90–91). In time, Whitman learned to face the noise and the stench and the suffering. "The first shudder has long past over," he wrote to Emerson after the initial couple of weeks were gone by (*Correspondence,* p. 99). To his brother Jeff, Walt wrote, "I never before had my feelings so thoroughly and so permanently absorbed, to the very roots, as by these huge swarms of dear, wounded, sick, dying boys—I get very much attached to some of them, and many of them have come to depend on seeing me, and having me sit by them a few minutes, as if for their lives" (*Correspondence,* p. 101).

Walt brought gifts. He came to the hospitals almost daily with candy, chewing gum, tobacco, wine, brandy, shirts, and socks. He gave the men letter-writing supplies, pens and paper. If a man didn't know how to write, Whitman took dictation. If a man was too sick or injured to pick up a pencil, Whitman picked it up for him. Because of Whitman, many families were delivered from anguish, learning that their boys were still alive. He did the soldiers' bidding as well as he could. A German boy, dying, asked for a Lutheran clergyman. Whitman went out through the streets of Washington and found one (*Correspondence,* pp. 104–105). A young man named Henry Boardman was sick of hospital food. "What would you like?" Whitman asked. "Rice pudding." Whitman had some made for him.

These small gifts cost money. Whitman used and sometimes used up his salary from the paymaster's office where he was clerking. There was always need for more. Walt got his brother Jeff to take up a collection back home in New York, and in came a few dollars. Whitman also wrote for pay. He composed a piece called "The Great Army of the Sick," published it in the *New York Times,* and gathered a few dollars more for his men and boys. "Reader," he says in that piece, "how can I describe to you the mute appealing look that rolls and moves from many a manly eye, from many a sick cot, following you as you walk slowly down one of those wards? To see these, and be incapable of responding to them, except in a few cases (so very few compared to the whole of the suffering men), is enough to make one's heart crack" ("The Great Army of the Sick," February 26, 1863, p. 107, *Walt Whitman Archive,* accessed August 13, 2020). The piece was so well received that the publisher sent Whitman an extra fifty dollars, much of which he surely put to use buying the men what they needed.

LETTERS HOME

Whitman chronicled his time in the hospital in a remarkable series of letters, many of them written to his mother, Louisa. A few were to Ralph Waldo Emerson, his teacher—though now his pupil too. Walt sent these lines to Emerson when he first came to the hospitals: "I desire and intend to write a little book out of this phase of America, her masculine young manhood, its conduct under most trying of and highest of all exigency, which she, as by lifting a corner in a curtain, has vouchsafed me to see America, already brought to Hospital in her fair youth— brought and deposited here in this great, whited sepulcher of Washington itself" (*Correspondence,* p. 69). Along with the soldiers, there came to Washington a wave of office seekers, profiteers, and all-around hustlers: "well-drest, rotten, meagre, nimble and impotent, full of gab" (p. 69). To Walt, they made a potent contrast to the soldiers. "This other freight of helpless worn and wounded youth, genuine of the soil, of darlings and true heirs to me the first unquestioned and convincing western crop, prophetic of the future, proofs undeniable to all men's ken of perfect beauty, tenderness and pluck that never race yet rivalled" (p. 69). Whitman did not care at all for the creatures who descended on Washington for gain. But from the start, he adored the soldiers for their valor, simplicity, and stoicism.

Ostensibly, Walt had a job when he was in Washington. Emerson had written him a letter of recommendation, and in not long Walt was installed in the office of Major Lyman Hapgood. The poet worked mornings copying government documents for the major, work that was dull enough but not terribly demanding. Walt was capable of very hard work, but he was also expert at loafing and lazing around. He seems to have acquitted himself reasonably well at Hapgood's office, but it's also clear that when he felt it was time to get up from his desk and wander off to other business, he did.

What Whitman faced when he entered the hospitals was daunting by anyone's measure. The letter to Emerson continues:

> Here in their barracks they lie—in those boarded Washington hospital barracks, whitewashed outside and in, one story, high enough, airy and clean enough—one of the Wards, for sample, a long stretch, a hundred and sixty feet long, with aisle down the middle, with cots, fifty or more on each side—and Death there up and down the aisle, tapping lightly by night or day here and there some poor young man, with relieving touch—that is one Ward, a cluster of ten or twelve make a current Washington Hospital—wherein this moment lie languishing, burning with fever or down with diarrhea, the imperial blood and rarest marrow of the North. (p. 70)

To describe the scene, Walt drew on his journalistic powers: he gives one the feel of the barrack, "high and airy," and the relevant facts: the aisles a hundred and sixty feet long; the cots fifty to a side. But Walt the poet enters in too: "Death . . . up and down the aisle, tapping lightly by night or day." The men are the "*imperial* blood and rarest marrow of the North." Is it a mistake on Walt's part to use feudal language to describe them? (*Imperium* is Latin for "empire.") Is it like giving the little captain those battle-lantern eyes in *Song*? Maybe. Walt is trying to create a new language for democratic heroism—an enormous task—and it's no wonder that he doesn't always succeed. But then perhaps Walt feels that the language of the old feudal days now belongs by right to the democracy, so strongly is it showing its superiority.

Walt continues: "here, at any rate, I go for a couple hours daily, and get to be welcome and useful, I find the masses fully justified by closest contact, never vulgar, ever calm, without greediness, no flummery, no frivolity—responding electric and without fail to affection, yet no whining—not the first unmanly whimper have I yet seen or heard" (p. 70). These were the kinds of Americans Whitman had dreamed of in *Song of Myself*, proud and self-reliant—a people, he believed, like none other in the world. He was not surprised that many of them came from the West, where he felt America was rejuvenating itself, overcoming the corruption of the East. He called them "true heirs" to himself, for finally perhaps he was finding not an audience for his poems but a manifestation of the sort of American people he had envisioned in them.

To him, these men were doing what he'd hoped Americans would in time do, eclipsing the heroes of the ancient world. They were not the product of Homer and Virgil but of the Declaration and the Constitution. Not long after his arrival, Whitman wrote:

> Got very much interested in some particular cases in Hospitals here—go now steadily to more or less of said Hospitals by day or night—find always the sick and dying soldiers forthwith begin to cling to me in a way that makes a fellow feel funny enough. These Hospitals, so different from all others—these thousands, and tens and twenties of thousands of American young men, badly wounded, all sorts of wounds, operated on, pallid with diarrhea, languishing, dying with fever, pneumonia, &c. open a new world somehow to me, giving closer insights, new things, exploring deeper mines than any yet, showing our humanity. (*Correspondence,* p. 81)

Walt the poet finds new insight into the human condition; Walt the patriot sees the triumph of democratic values in the men around him. The democratic humanitarian sees a chance to help.

"To these scenes," he writes, "what are your dramas and poems, even the oldest and the tearfulest? Not old Greek mighty ones, where man contends with fate, (and always yields)—not Virgil showing Dante on and on among the agonized & damned, approach what here I see and take a part in. For here I see, not at intervals, but quite always, how certain, our American man—how he holds himself cool and unquestioned master above all pains and bloody mutilations. It is immense, the best thing of all, nourishes me of all men" (*Correspondence,* pp. 81–82).

Whitman wasn't only finding American heroes to challenge the heroes of the old, feudal civilizations. He was also discovering new powers in himself. It seems he could do in life what he imagined in his poetry: he could enter the spirits of the wounded men who surround him. He says, "[They] open a new world somehow to me, giving closer insights." But he had seen a preview of that new world in his vision of 1854 and 1855, when he had become the mashed fireman, the hounded slave, the old artillerist. "I am the man," he wrote then. "I suffered . . . . I was there" (SoM, l. 827).

Whitman came to believe that he was a transforming influence on the soldiers, a healing presence:

> I adapt myself to each case. Some need to be humored, some are rather out of their head—some merely want me to sit down [near] them, & hold them by the hand—one will want a letter written to mother or father, (yesterd[ay] I wrote over a dozen letters)—some like to have me feed them (wounded perhaps in shoulder or wrist) perhaps a few bits of my peaches—some want a cooling drink, (I have some very nice syrups from raspberries &c.)—others want writing paper, envelopes, a stamp, &c.—I could fill a sheet with one day's items—I often go, just at dark, sometimes stay nearly all night—I like to go just before supper, carrying a pot or jar of something good & go around with a spoon distributing a little here and there. (*Correspondence,* pp. 101–102)

But he gave more than practical help. "After all this succoring of the stomach (which is of course most welcome & indispensable) I should say that I believe my profoundest help to these sick & dying men is probably the soothing invigoration I steadily bear in mind, to infuse in them through affection, cheering love, & the like, between them & me. It has saved more than one life. There is a strange influence here. I have formed attachments here in hospital, that I shall keep to my dying day, & they will the same, without doubt" (*Correspondence,* p. 102). Whitman formed his attachments, and the men grew attached to him as well. His presence surely saved more than one life.

Whitman thought constantly about the boys and men, but he thought about himself and his own presence too. When his clothes were wearing down, his mother, Louisa, who had little enough money, sent him new shirts. The poet was delighted: "O mother, how welcome the shirts were—I was putting off, & putting off, to get some new ones, I could not find any one to do them as I wear them, & it would have cost such a price" (*Correspondence,* p. 102). He told Louisa that his old clothes were nothing but rags, held together with starch.

Walt also acquired a new suit: "a nice plain suit, of a dark wine color, looks very well, & feels good, single breasted sack coat with breast pockets &c. & vest & pants same as what I always wear, (pants pretty full,) so upon the whole all looks unusually good for me, my hat is very good yet, boots ditto, have a new necktie, nice shirts" (*Correspondence,* p. 103). Walt tells Louisa that he hasn't trimmed his beard since he was home in Brooklyn and that though it hasn't grown any longer, it's now quite a bit bushier than it was. Walt's as stout as ever, around two hundred pounds. He eats well and copiously. Altogether, he tells his mother, "I cut quite a swell." He produces a "sufficient sensation." His health? He tells Louisa that he's never felt better (p. 103).

Walt understood the value of his art and worked hard to perfect what he'd written. But he also knew the value of appearances. In New York, during the Broadway days, he took pains to look the part of the poet. Now in Washington, it matters a great deal to him to come across as healthy, robust, and manly. His flourishing beard is a sign of virile strength. His dress marks him out as an individualist; he's his own man, to be taken on respectful terms and not to be trifled with. Walt had been sculpting personae for himself at least from the days when he had that manly engraving inscribed at the front of *Leaves* and had Emerson's line about his great career embossed on the side of the 1856 volume. Beginning in middle age, Walt photographed wonderfully well. (He often looked *much* better than he felt.) And in time, it seems that he never met a camera he didn't like. (He posed at least once with what seemed a tame butterfly on his finger—though it was no more than a model.) He would do anything to get his poems out and into the world. Now he was crafting a persona as the virile healer—tough, eccentric, and warm. It gratified him, no doubt. It harked back to the days when he stopped before a store window on Broadway to take in his beautiful reflection and watch the crowd rush in torrents behind him. The self-adornment was gratifying to Walt, no doubt. But maybe it did something to buoy up his sick patients too.

Whitman quickly became a familiar and accepted figure in the hospitals. Everyone on the staff seemed to know him and let him make his way through the worst of the suffering. And the worst was very bad. "O mother," he writes, "there seems to me as I go through these rows of cots, as if it was too bad to accept these *children,* to subject them to such premature experiences—I devote myself much to Armory Square Hospital because it contains by far the worst cases, most repulsive wounds, has the most suffering & most need of consolation—I go every day without fail, & often at night—sometimes stay very late—no one interferes with me, guards, doctors, nurses, nor any one—I am let to take my own course" (*Correspondence,* p. 112). They are only children, these warriors—and Walt treats them with the dignity best accorded to brave men and the tenderness that all children deserve but in time of war rarely find.

Day after day, he continued on, doing small acts of kindness that meant worlds to the men. To a friend, probably James Redpath, he wrote, "I have been most of this day in Armory Square Hospital, Seventh st. I seldom miss a day or evening. Out of the six or seven hundred in this Hosp[ital] I try to give a word or a trifle to every one without exception, making regular rounds among them all. I give all kinds of sustenance, blackberries, peaches, lemons & sugar, wines, all kinds of preserves, pickles, brandy, milk, shirts, & all articles of underclothing, tobacco, tea, handkerchiefs, &c &c &c. I always give paper, envelopes, stamps, &c. I want to supply for this purpose" (*Correspondence,* p. 122). Six or seven hundred in a day: the degree of human and humane energy Walt needed for so many encounters overwhelms the imagination.

Whitman found that many of the men were completely broke. Their salaries, such as they were, never reached them. He saw how humiliating it was to be lying ill and wounded without a cent. He gave them his own money and did what he could to raise money from others. "To many I give (when I have it) small sums of money—half of the soldiers in hospital have not a cent. There are many returned prisoners, sick, lost all—& every day squads of men from [the] front, cavalry or infantry—brought in wounded or sick, generally without a cent of money" (*Correspondence,* p. 122). It didn't bother Walt to pass out almost everything he had. He'd been born poor and was certain he'd be poor all his life. Poverty was probably his preferred condition: money might tempt him to try to stand above other men and women.

Walt had a word and a small gift for most everyone in the hospitals. But he was particularly drawn to the worst casualties. His ability to face such suffering is nearly incomprehensible, until we remember that in his poetic vision, he had seen so much misery, as well as joy. "I pass death with the dying, and birth with the new-washed babe," he says. And there in the hospitals, he saw his share of death. But he also said he was "not contained between [his] hat and boots" (l. 124). That is, his presence was mystical, imaginative, and empathic, as well as physical. He connected with the soldiers, soul to soul. "I select the most needy cases & devote my time & services much to them. I find it tells best—some are mere lads, 17, 18, 19, or 20. Some are silent, sick, heavy hearted, (things, attentions, &c. are very rude in the army & hospitals, nothing but the mere hard routine, no time for tenderness or extras)—So I go round—Some of my boys die, some get well—" (*Correspondence,* p. 122) Some died, some got well—and Walt was there beside them, doing what he could. Whitman had something for everybody: he notes more than once that he did what he could for the Black troops and for the Confederate fighters as well. He was there for all.

His poetic vision had *readied* him for the hospitals, but over time his sense of his role as friend to the wounded and dying became deeper and more realistic. This is Walt in *Song:*

> To any one dying . . . . thither I speed and twist the knob of the door,
> Turn the bedclothes toward the foot of the bed,
> Let the physician and the priest go home.
>
> I seize the descending man . . . . I raise him with resistless will.
>
> O despairer, here is my neck,
> By God! you shall not go down! Hang your whole weight upon me.
>
> I dilate you with tremendous breath . . . . I buoy you up;
> Every room of the house do I fill with an armed force . . . . lovers of
>   me, bafflers of graves:
> Sleep! I and they keep guard all night;
> Not doubt, not decease shall dare to lay finger upon you,
> I have embraced you, and henceforth possess you to myself,
> And when you rise in the morning you will find what I tell you is
>   so. (ll. 1003–1014)

The vision here is intense and hyperbolic. Whitman assumes nearly supernatural powers of comfort and healing. Whatever grandiosity Walt may have felt on this score in 1854 and 1855, the actual experience of the hospitals changed him. His work there was patient, incremental, steady, kind, and often inflected with resignation. But that does not mean he did not save some lives, change the course of some human events, baffle a grave or two.

The work in the hospitals was difficult and draining. But from time to time Walt found ways to lighten the burden. He lived in a house with his friends, the O'Connors, and they became a second family to him. He and William O'Connor, novelist and abolitionist, walked late through the streets of Washington, talking about politics and literature and love. (O'Connor was something of a man about town.) Nellie, William's wife, was intelligent and principled, if a little dour, and enjoyed having Walt on the scene. She may even have fallen in love with him.

One New Year's Eve, Walt arrived at the O'Connor house looking like Santa Claus, with snow sprinkled on his beard, hat, and shoulders. In his sack were a bottle of Scotch, a lemon, and some lumps of sugar. Walt said that he was going to make a hot punch to his own precise specifications. The water came off the stove the moment it boiled; each lemon chunk was of exactly the same dimension, and every glass got a sugar lump, just the right size. It must have felt to Walt like the old days at Pfaff's (Allen, p. 301).

There were warm, congenial moments in Washington, but then it was back to the hospitals. Sometimes when one of the soldiers died, Walt wrote to the soldier's parents and told them about his last hours. These were not easy letters to write, but how much they must have meant to the families of the young men. Here is a portion of one, sent to the parents of Erastus Haskell:

> Many nights I sat in the hospital by his bedside till far in the night—The lights would be put out—yet I would sit there silently, hours, late, perhaps fanning him—he always liked to have me sit there, but never cared to talk—I shall never forget those nights, it was a curious & solemn scene, the sick & wounded lying around in their cots, just visible in the darkness, & this dear man close at hand lying on what proved to be his death bed—I do not know his past life, but what I do know, & what I saw of him, he was a noble boy—I felt he was one I should get very much attached to. I think you have reason to be proud of such a son, & all his relatives have cause to treasure his memory. (*Correspondence,* p. 129)

Whitman wants Erastus's parents to remember his last hours. He wants to be precise and detailed about their boy. Walt continues:

> Poor dear son, though you were not my son, I felt to love you as a son, what short time I saw you sick & dying here—it is as well as it is, perhaps better—for who knows whether he is not better off, that patient & sweet young soul, to go, than we are to stay? So farewell, dear boy—it was my opportunity to be with you in your last rapid days of death—no chance as I have said to do any thing in particular, for nothing [could be done—only you did not lie] here & die among strangers without having one at hand who loved you dearly, & to whom you gave your dying kiss—" (p. 129)

Remember this: the greatest and most original writer that America has ever produced spent time writing letters in behalf of young men to their grieving parents. If in all of literary history there is an example of comparable largesse of spirit, I do not know where it's to be found.

Walt maintained his integrity in the letters he wrote to the soldiers' parents. He did not talk about God or the afterlife—though he was willing to say that we could not know the future of the departed ones. When one of the wounded or dying men spoke to Walt about faith in divine Jesus and the Lord God, Walt treated the man with kind respect, but never falsely joined him in his convictions. Walt let the men know that he was glad for their faith—and that was all. In *Specimen Days,* he recalls how a soldier named Oscar F. Wilber of the 154th New York Regiment asked him to read to him from the Bible. Walt could see that Oscar was dying, and he read to him about the last hours of Christ and the crucifixion, which brought the young man to tears. "He asked me," Walt says, "if I enjoyed religion. 'Perhaps not my dear, in the way you mean, and yet may-be it is the same thing'" (LoA, p. 731).

Whitman cared about others who worked in the hospitals too. He came to know Miss Gregg, who felt that her efforts, boundless as they may have been, were not appreciated. Walt wrote to let her know that wasn't so. She'd made a difference:

> Dear friend, You spoke the other day, partly in fun, about the men being so undemonstrative. I thought I would write you a line, as I

hear you leave the hospital tomorrow for a few weeks. Your labor of love & disinterestedness here in Hospital is appreciated. I have invariably heard the Ward A patients speak of you with gratitude, sometimes with enthusiasm. They have their own ways (not outside éclat, but in manly American hearts, however rude, however undemonstrative to you). I thought it would be sweet to your tender & womanly heart, to know what I have so often heard from the soldiers about you, as I sat by their sick cots. I too have learnt to love you, seeing your tender heart, & your goodness to those wounded & dying young men—for they have grown to seem to me as my sons or dear young brothers. (*Correspondence,* p. 143)

Walt says that he would like to give her a present, yet he is too poor. "But I write you this note, dear girl, knowing you will receive it in the same candor & good faith it is written" (p. 143). Walt was poor in material things but rich in compassion and kindness.

Maybe the most charming of all Walt's gestures was going out to get ice cream and distributing it to men who'd never had any before: "O I must tell you," he wrote to Louisa, "I gave the boys in Carver hospital a great treat of ice cream a couple of days ago, went round myself through about 15 large wards, (I bought some ten gallons, very nice)—you would have cried & been amused too, many of the men had to be fed, several of them I saw cannot probably live, yet they quite enjoyed it, I gave everybody some—quite a number western country boys had never tasted ice cream before—they relish such things, oranges, lemons, &c" (*Correspondence,* p. 230).

But the darkness was always close. Walt never denied or tried to evade it. He continued, "Mother, I feel a little blue this morning, as two young men I knew very well have just died, one died last night, & the other about half an hour before I went to the hospital, I did not anticipate the death of either of them, each was a very, very sad case, so young—well, mother, I see I have written you another gloomy sort of letter—I do not feel as first rate as usual" (p. 230). The hospitals are beginning to wear on Walt. He had always been proud of his great good health, but now it was beginning, just beginning, to fail.

TOM SAWYER

In the hospitals, Walt Whitman fell in love. His beloved's name was Tom Sawyer, the name Mark Twain would give to his feckless good-bad boy. Walt's Tom Sawyer was a patient in one of the Washington hospitals, but by the time we hear about him in the letters, he's been discharged. On April 26, 1863, Walt wrote to Tom to say:

> I have not heard from you for some time, Lewy Brown has received two letters from you, & Walter in Ward E has received one three weeks ago. I wrote you a letter about a week ago, which I hope you have received. I was sorry you did not come up to my room to get the shirt & other things you promised to accept from me and take when you went away. I got them all ready, a good strong blue shirt, a pair of drawers & socks, and it would have been a satisfaction to me if you had accepted them. I should have often thought now Tom may be wearing around his body something from *me,* & that it might contribute to your comfort, down there in camp on picket, or sleeping in your tent. (*Correspondence,* p. 93)

The tone of exasperation that begins the letter—why, why didn't you write me?—is uncommon in Whitman. He's usually genial and undemanding. Whitman's feeling for Tom is nearly maternal in this letter—son, you need some good warm clothes. Still, the line about coming up to Walt's room suggests a hope for intimacy and maybe something adventurous.

The letter goes on to reveal a pining Walt Whitman:

> Tom, I will not write a long yarn at present. I guess I have not made out much of a letter, anyhow at present, but I will let it go, whatever

it is, hoping it may please you, coming from old wooly-neck, who loves you. You must let that make up for all deficiencies now and to come. Not a day passes, nor a night but I think of you. Now, my dearest comrade, I will bid you *so long,* & hope God will put it in your heart to bear toward me a little at least of the feeling I have about you. If it is only a quarter as much I shall be satisfied. (pp. 93–94)

This is the sound of deep unrequited love. And of course the recourse to God is uncharacteristic—suggesting how desperate Walt was to connect with Tom.

About Tom Sawyer personally, we know little. We know that he served in the 111th Massachusetts Infantry and that he incurred his wounds at the Second Battle of Bull Run in August 1862. He was in his early twenties, and came from Cambridgeport, Massachusetts, where he had worked as a soap maker. Whitman spent hours talking to Tom and his friend Lewy Brown in the hospitals. They laughed and swapped stories and probably engaged in long games of twenty questions, one of Walt's favorite diversions. Tom did eventually communicate with Whitman, though he did so through Lewy Brown. Something of Tom's simplicity and kindness comes through in the note: "I want you to give my love to Walter Whitman and tell him that I am very sorry that I could not live up to my Prommice because I came away so soon that it sliped my mind and I am very sorry for it, tell him that I shall write to him my self in a few days, give him my love and best wishes for ever" (*Correspondence,* p. 90n86). It was eight months before Tom actually wrote to Whitman, a stiff and formal note that must have wounded Walt badly.

Walt's love and longing grow over time. "My dearest comrade, I cannot, though I attempt it, put in a letter the feelings of my heart—i suppose my letters sound strange & unusual to you as it is, but as I am only expressing the truth in them, I do not trouble myself on that account. As I intimated before, I do not expect you to return for me the same degree of love I have for you" (*Correspondence,* p. 107). Walt is beyond abject—he will accept almost any kind of contact from his beloved.

Writing to their mutual friend Lewy Brown, Walt says, "Lew, when you write to Tom Sawyer you know what to say from me—he is one I love in my heart, & always shall till death, & afterwards too" (*Correspondence*, p. 181). And then there is a final cry in a letter to Tom himself, after Tom's long silence:

> Well, comrade, I must close. I do not know why you do not write to me. Do you wish to shake me off? That I cannot believe, for I have the same love for you that I exprest in my letters last spring, & I am confident you have the same for me. Anyhow I go on my own gait, & wherever I am in this world, while I have a meal, or a dollar, or if I should have some shanty of my own, no living man will ever be more welcome there than Tom Sawyer. So good by, dear comrade, & God bless you, & if fortune should keep you from me here, in this world, it must not hereafter. (*Correspondence,* p. 186)

Walt is so distressed here that he again breaks one of his most stalwart rules: he reflects on a possible life after death in Christian terms.

It's worth noting that Tom Sawyer is never there on the scene with Walt. He's an absent presence, an object of desire partly real, partly created by Walt's imagination. And how could Walt not have been tempted by the prospect of settling down and enjoying one love? Why shouldn't he possess what nearly everyone else can? In a poem called "I Saw in Louisiana a Live-Oak Growing," Walt talks about the strains of not having his beloved, his special comrade present with him:

> I saw in Louisiana a live-oak growing,
> All alone stood it and the moss hung down from the branches,
> Without any companion it grew there uttering joyous leaves of dark
>   green,
> And its look, rude unbending, lusty, made me think of myself,
> But I wondered how it could utter joyous leaves standing alone there
>   without its friend near, for I knew I could not. (LoA, p. 279)

The tree, Walt says, makes him think of "manly love": "I broke off a twig with a certain number of leaves upon it and twined around it a little moss, / And brought it away, and I have placed it in sight of my room" (p. 280). It's hard not to see Walt's keepsake as a phallic emblem, something that reminds him of more than manly love of the platonic sort. At the end of the poem, Walt looks wonderingly at the tree "uttering joyous leaves all its life without a friend a lover near, / I knew very well I could not" (p. 280).

Overall the poem conveys pining for mutual and exclusive love with another. The tree can produce its leaves in solitude, but Walt doubts his power to "utter" his own "joyous leaves"—his poems—without having someone he deeply loves close by him.

At least at times, Walt wants what most all of us want—mutual love, human response from one special being. But in his poetry and in much of his life, he was committed to multiplicity. He wanted to stay on the move, get to the open road, ramble from place to place, person to person. It's not surprising that the urge to have what others do sometimes took possession of him. Would he have succumbed to being a couple, a nation of two, if Tom had said yes? It's impossible to know. The more important question is whether one can live the democratic life that Walt wanted without giving up on exclusive love. Can you be a Whitmanian democrat, warm friend to each and all, and sustain a life of personal intimacy with a wife or husband or beloved? Can the Whitmanian wanderer thrive in a family?

It seems to me almost inevitable that Whitman's spiritual democracy, in which the individual does all possible to love every member of the nation, would have to weaken exclusive bonds. People in this dispensation might still marry, but there would be few if any nations of two. Energies would be needed elsewhere. And what would happen to the children? How well could their parents—comrades to all—take care of them?

When we look back into *Song*, we see that Walt isn't averse to wedded love. He celebrates the marriage of the trapper and the American Indian girl. And there are scenes of joyful family life. Walt does, at one point, describe himself as turning a bridegroom out of bed and clutching the bride all through the night, an aggressive slap at marriage and an assertion, we might say, of *droit du poète*. ("I turn the bridegroom out of bed and stay with the bride myself, / And tighten her all night to my thighs and lips" [ll. 814–815].) The question of marriage and mutually exclusive love is one that seems to me to stand unresolved in Walt's vision.

Walt tells us constantly in *Song* that the work of imagining spiritual democracy is anything but finished. He enjoins us repeatedly to take up where he leaves off and carry the vision forward. And on this question, the question of mutual love, there is considerable Whitman-inspired work to do.

In time, the work in the hospital got to Whitman, despite his formidable strength. He grew sick. He may have suffered a mild stroke, then another. Not long after he delivered the ice cream to the men from the Midwest, Walt told his mother that he was not feeling his best: "Mother, I have not felt well at all the last week—I had spells of deathly faintness, and bad trouble in my head too, & sore throat, (quite a little budget, ain't they?)—My head was the worst, though I don't know, the faint weak spells were not very pleasant—but I feel so much better this forenoon I believe it has passed over" (*Correspondence,* p. 231). Walt is complaining about his own situation, which he rarely does at any time in his life. But then it's quickly on to the men: "There is a very horrible collection in Armory Building, (in Armory Square hosp.) about 200 of the worst cases you ever see, & I had been probably too much with them—it is enough to melt the heart of a stone—over one third of them are amputation cases" (p. 231). The question isn't why Walt is now beginning to get ill but how he stayed healthy for so long.

On June 10, he writes, "I feel a good deal better this morning, I go around, but most of the time feel very little like it—the doctor tells me I have continued too long in the hospitals, especially in a bad place, armory building, where the worst wounds were, & have absorbed too much of the virus in my system—but I know it is nothing but what a little relief & sustenance of right sort, will set right—" (*Correspondence,* p. 233). Walt does his best to recuperate and take some time for himself, but he finds that he cannot stay away from the wounded and dying men.

At last he has to admit that the hospitals are undoing his once-powerful constitution:

> I am not feeling very well these days—the doctors have told me not to come inside the hospitals for the present—I send there by a friend every day, I send things & aid to some cases I know, & hear from there also, but I do not go myself at present—it is probable that the hospital poison has affected my system, & I find it worse than I calculated—I have spells of faintness & very bad feeling in my head, fullness & pain—& besides sore throat—my boarding place, 502 Pennsylvania av, is a miserable place, very bad air—But I shall feel

better soon, I know—the doctors say it will pass over—they have long told me I was going in too strong—some days I think it has all gone & I feel well again, but in a few hours I have a spell again—(p. 233)

But Walt keeps on coming. Even when the war is over, he continues on in Washington, visiting his hospitals, doing what he can.

THE VISION COMPLETED

In Washington, at the hospitals, Whitman effectively completed *Song of Myself*. He became a version of the individual that his poem prophesied.

He engaged his soul, "clear and sweet," as he called it. His soul became his medium of connection with the sick, wounded, and dying men. His spiritual imagination allowed him to see who they were, what they were feeling, and how he could help them. All of his imaginative mergers in the poem—the fireman, the hounded slave, the old artillerist, Jesus— were rehearsals for the way he entered into the hearts of the young men. The tender figure that Walt brought forth at the start of *Song*, compassionating, idle, and unitary, was in a sense there in Washington, looking on with its side-curved head, sympathizing with all. Walt's Soul loved beyond measure in the hospitals.

In the hospitals, he was also Walt Whitman, one of the roughs. He was tough. Whitman's endurance during the hospital years was astounding. He worked hour past hour, day after day, in a horrible environment, doing all he could. His health was always in jeopardy, but somehow he held up for more than two years. In the hospitals, Whitman proved to be durable and strong. He truly possessed what Emerson said he did: "buffalo strength." He showed that when a person allows himself full access to his vulnerable Soul, he doesn't have to become weak and easily discouraged. In the hospitals, Walt was still that formidable man in the engraving at the beginning of *Leaves*. Yet he was more than that too.

Whitman didn't bring God into the hospitals with him. Preachers of all stripes made their ways to the wards, bent on shoring up the men's faith or converting them. Whitman did no such thing. The soldiers knew and loved him as the man who did not preach to them. He may have gone on beholding God in every object, but he did not surrender the idea that he—and all others in the democracy—were as marvelous as God could ever be and maybe more so. The Hegelian-American passages in *Song* had brought Walt to the point where he did not despise religion or priests. But he understood that the priests and religions were a prelude. They helped make possible what we could have here in America, the spiritualization of democracy. Some of their work was to be applauded. Hurrah for them. But now they were outmoded, and needed to be put in binders and placed on the shelf. A new age was at hand, one in which we could see (with Walt's help) that all of what was best in religion had simply led up to the spiritual democracy that was coming into being.

When Walt was in the hospitals, he kept moving—man to man, bed to bed, ward to ward, hospital to hospital. His poem had showed him what it was like to stay in motion, giving all the love he could muster to this one and that—then moving on, before he got caught or encumbered. Would he have succumbed to the lure of a life with Lewy Brown or the beloved Tom Sawyer if he'd had the chance? We can never know. But I think not. Whitman was all for the road—in this case the long road, endless it no doubt seemed, that ran down the center of the hospital wards.

He included everyone in his hospital ministrations, as *Song* promised that he would. Union soldiers and Confederates, Black and White, young and middle aged: if you were in the hospital, Whitman was there to help you. Walt was friendly to everyone and took people on equal terms. Remember, he did not want to be extraordinary—he was one of the mass, one of the group. His job was poet. Yours might be blacksmith, tinker or weaver, or soldier. You all did your best with pride. No one was better than anyone else. If you told Walt that he was extraordinary, wonderful, grand, he could well have been offended. He was one of the crowd, a citizen in the great experiment.

In the hospitals, Walt was able to look straight at death. He could do this in a way that almost no one who is not a doctor or nurse can. But his vision had prepared him for. it. "To die is different from what any one supposed, and luckier," he said (SoM, l. 121). Whitman knew that he was a blade of grass and that he would be reincarnated as fresh grass—new citizens of the democracy—arose in the world. "The smallest sprout shows there is really no death" (l. 117). He must have believed this: it had been revealed to him in his vision. If not, he couldn't have faced death, both his own death—he risked his life every day in the hospitals—and the deaths of so many soldiers, with as much equanimity as he did, then come back the next day and the next day to give more help.

Whitman didn't do his good deeds under anyone's direction but his own. He didn't care for bosses or doctors or ward overseers. No suns or aspiring suns for him. For a while he was associated with relief agencies, but their members did not care for him, nor he for them. Quietly and modestly he went about his business, putting into practice what he had learned from the spiritual voyage he had undertaken. And the men came to love him, as much as he did them.

In his vision, Whitman had seen war: he'd been at an old-time sea fight and present at the jet-black sunrise. He wasn't afraid of violence, and he knew it to be necessary for sustaining democracy. He didn't pull back or turn away—he understood that battle was part of human life. He risked his life in the hospitals day to day almost as much as the soldiers did at the front.

Through his actions in the hospitals, Walt addressed one of the major unresolved problems of *Song of Myself*. Who is talking here? How shall we understand this author? Is he one of "the supremes," as he half-jokingly suggests? Is he a fierce Nietzschean teacher who believes that his students become themselves by turning against or even destroying him? Or is he a tuft of grass under our bootsoles?

I think that the question of authority that brought Whitman to poetic confusion at the end *Song*—and as apparently casual as he is, Walt is rarely anything but consistent—is resolved in the hospitals. There Whitman assumes a true humility. He shows us that he does not think himself better than others, a supreme. And he offers a suggestion of how democratic "heroes" should comport themselves. They can become humble and serve the people, become modest and kind. They can show the world, and show themselves, that they are just one of the mass, a part of the great random. Elevated? Put on high? Tempted to think of yourself as one of the elect? Off to the hospital, the soup kitchen, the slum, the faltering school, the shelter for the victims. Walt showed the way. He posed the question of authority and status in the poem. He answered it in the hospitals.

It is very hard to imagine, at least for me, the capacity to achieve what Walt did as an artist, then to turn and make oneself as humble as he was in the hospitals. One thinks of Emerson's perception that real achievement requires self-assertion and even competition with the rest. The desire to hold the first cultural place goes back to the Romans and Greeks, and who knows that it might not be an aspect of our human nature? Understanding that the reward of greatness is not high distinction, a standing over the rest, but self-humbling will not be easy, if it is possible at all. It may simply be too much for almost all of us, here and now. But perhaps with the passing of time, we'll see that Walt knows our powers better than we know them ourselves. Maybe we can be great and humble. Maybe we can love our fellow citizens fully and have enough left to take care of our children. Maybe we can walk Walt's path a little further than we might have imagined. One never knows without trying.

I would speculate that in formulating his answer to the questions of greatness and authority, Walt took inspiration from a fellow American he frequently saw in the streets of Washington during the war years, Abraham Lincoln. Whitman was fascinated by the president beginning that day in 1861 when he caught a look at him from the top of the Broadway stagecoach. In Washington, out walking early, Walt often saw Lincoln, walking himself, his countenance full of worry, sometimes woe. For a moment, perhaps the two greatest Americans of their time were present together. They saluted each other with a tip of the cap. Walt says that they got so that they exchanged bows and cordial ones, though never a word.

Whitman was a rebellious person, sweetly rebellious, and he did not usually care for leaders—whom he sometimes called Big Bugs. ("Resist much. Obey little.") His view of Lincoln was different. Walt admired his intellect and his verbal powers and his skills as a politician. But he also clearly admired Lincoln's humility. The president understood that steering the nation successfully through the Civil War was a task that was probably beyond any living human being. Still, the task was his, and he would do his best. He struggled with all the important decisions—who should command the army, how the draft should work, if this or that young man caught sleeping on sentry duty should face the firing squad. He knew he was fallible, and he was always worried about being wrong. Yet he made the decisions and moved forward. Whitman saw in Lincoln a man who understood his limits and respected them, despite being the most powerful person in America. In Lincoln, Whitman saw true modesty. The greatest poet in America and the greatest president had this in common—they were humble men.

And this, I believe, is the heart of democratic greatness, which in Whitman's case is a paradox but not a contradiction in terms. In democracy, we have our leaders, our remarkable artists, our creative scientists, our true thinkers. But they must attempt to be humble, as Whitman did: one of the bunch, just another everyday person. It's a terribly demanding standard. Who does not want to revel in success and achievement? But Whitman brought it off, and to his mind, Lincoln did too. In the first great catalogue, Walt depicted a prostitute: she "draggles her shawl, her bonnet bobs on her tipsy and pimpled neck,"

> The crowd laugh at her blackguard oaths, the men jeer and wink to
>   each other,
> (Miserable! I do not laugh at your oaths nor jeer you.) (SoM, ll.
>   303–304)

Then the poet moves on. The next figure in the catalogue is the president, who "holds a cabinet council, he is surrounded by the great secretaries" (l. 305). I believe that Lincoln would not have been at all offended appearing next to the prostitute. He would have seen it as a righteous emblem for true democracy. Like Walt, he would not have laughed; he would not have jeered.

Whitman wrote two consequential elegies for Lincoln, "When Lilacs Last in the Dooryard Bloom'd" and "O Captain! My Captain!" "O Captain! My Captain!" may be Whitman's most conventional poem: it's a ballad, and it equates Lincoln with the captain of a ship who has steered it effectively through storms. The ship, of course, is America; the storms, the Civil War. The poem is rather un-Whitmanian: it renders Lincoln as a hero who stands above others. All look to him in awe. Whitman was deeply ambivalent about "Captain." He read it at the climax of his famous yearly lecture on Lincoln, from which he gathered much of the money that kept him afloat the other 364 days. As the moment approached, the crowd would begin to clamor for the poem. And then, with great and understandable reluctance, Walt delivered it.

In "Lilacs," Whitman came up with a far more effective image for Lincoln than a ship's captain. There the fallen president is the "powerful western fallen star" (LoA, p. 459). The star, when it was bright and ascendant, surely gave guidance to the people below. But unlike the captain, who holds the power of office and gives commands, you follow the star only if you wish to. Your connection to it is volitional. It's a brilliant and moving image of Lincoln, entirely in keeping with Walt's implicit vision of democratic greatness.

Whitman brooded on Abraham Lincoln all through his life. For a long time, he doesn't seem to feel that he quite understands the martyred president. Finally, in an essay published in *November Boughs,* Whitman arrives at his deepest condensed thought about Lincoln. There Walt reflects on what he takes to be Lincoln's dual nature. "I should say the invisible foundations and vertebra of his character, more than any man's in history, were mystical, abstract, moral and spiritual" (LoA, p. 1198). Lincoln possessed spirit, depth, inwardness. But the great president had more. Upon his spiritual qualities "was built, and out of all of them radiated, under the control of the average of circumstances, what the vulgar call *horse sense,* and a life often bent by temporary but most urgent materialistic and political reasons" (p. 1198). In Lincoln, Whitman sees a reflection of his own complex being, brought to birth in the 1855 volume. Like Whitman, Lincoln is worldly, tough, and practical. But he's also inspired by ideals. He embodies a marriage of Self and Soul.

And Whitman? I like to think that the author of *Leaves of Grass* is the man who let his poem teach him how to live. The voyage he went on taught him to walk away from ambition and striving. It brought him into the hospitals, where he humbled himself in a way that few people can. We might say he became a servant to the democracy, clear and sweet and kind. Whitman's poem and his life in the hospitals set a standard for democratic thought and action, a high standard. Surely few of us could ever fulfill it. But I think he points us in the right direction, toward a genuine form of democratic happiness.

Who is Walt Whitman? He's the old man with the spuming beard fanning the dying boy over there. He's the one writing that armless young man's letter home. He's there, over there, laughing with the nurse, teasing the doctor, trying to draw a little more attention to the boy in the corner down with typhus. He's just come onto the ward, laughing, with vats of ice cream in both hands. There he is. He is the one who wrote the best American poem, *Song of Myself.* And then, and then, he's the one the great poem brought into being. He's up ahead waiting for us.

PART III

Song of Myself

(1855)

SONG OF MYSELF

I CELEBRATE myself,
And what I assume you shall assume,
For every atom belonging to me as good belongs to you.

I loafe and invite my soul,
I lean and loafe at my ease . . . . observing a spear of summer grass.   5

Houses and rooms are full of perfumes . . . . the shelves are crowded
   with perfumes,
I breathe the fragrance myself, and know it and like it,
The distillation would intoxicate me also, but I shall not let it.

The atmosphere is not a perfume . . . . it has no taste of the
   distillation . . . . it is odorless,
It is for my mouth forever . . . . I am in love with it,   10
I will go to the bank by the wood and become undisguised and naked,
I am mad for it to be in contact with me.

The smoke of my own breath,
Echos, ripples, and buzzed whispers . . . . loveroot, silkthread, crotch
   and vine,
My respiration and inspiration . . . . the beating of my heart . . . . the
   passing of blood and air through my lungs,   15
The sniff of green leaves and dry leaves, and of the shore and
   darkcolored sea-rocks, and of hay in the barn,

The sound of the belched words of my voice . . . . words loosed to the
    eddies of the wind,
A few light kisses . . . . a few embraces . . . . a reaching around of arms,
The play of shine and shade on the trees as the supple boughs wag,
The delight alone or in the rush of the streets, or along the fields and
20   hillsides,
The feeling of health . . . . the full-noon trill . . . . the song of me rising
    from bed and meeting the sun.

Have you reckoned a thousand acres much? Have you reckoned the
    earth much?
Have you practiced so long to learn to read?
Have you felt so proud to get at the meaning of poems?

Stop this day and night with me and you shall possess the origin of all
25   poems,
You shall possess the good of the earth and sun . . . . there are millions
    of suns left,
You shall no longer take things at second or third hand . . . . nor
    look through the eyes of the dead . . . . nor feed on the spectres in
    books,
You shall not look through my eyes either, nor take things from me,
You shall listen to all sides and filter them from yourself.

I have heard what the talkers were talking . . . . the talk of the
30   beginning and the end,
But I do not talk of the beginning or the end.

There was never any more inception than there is now,
Nor any more youth or age than there is now;
And will never be any more perfection than there is now,
35 Nor any more heaven or hell than there is now.

Urge and urge and urge,
Always the procreant urge of the world.

Out of the dimness opposite equals advance . . . . Always substance and
    increase,
Always a knit of identity . . . . always distinction . . . . always a breed
    of life.

To elaborate is no avail . . . . Learned and unlearned feel that it is so.   40

Sure as the most certain sure . . . . plumb in the uprights, well entretied,
    braced in the beams,
Stout as a horse, affectionate, haughty, electrical,
I and this mystery here we stand.

Clear and sweet is my soul . . . . and clear and sweet is all that is not
    my soul.

Lack one lacks both . . . . and the unseen is proved by the seen,   45
Till that becomes unseen and receives proof in its turn.

Showing the best and dividing it from the worst, age vexes age,
Knowing the perfect fitness and equanimity of things, while they
    discuss I am silent, and go bathe and admire myself.

Welcome is every organ and attribute of me, and of any man hearty
    and clean,
Not an inch nor a particle of an inch is vile, and none shall be less
    familiar than the rest.   50

I am satisfied . . . . I see, dance, laugh, sing;
As God comes a loving bedfellow and sleeps at my side all night and
    close on the peep of the day,
And leaves for me baskets covered with white towels bulging the house
    with their plenty,
Shall I postpone my acceptation and realization and scream at my
    eyes,

55 That they turn from gazing after and down the road,
    And forthwith cipher and show me to a cent,
    Exactly the contents of one, and exactly the contents of two, and which
        is ahead?

    Trippers and askers surround me,
    People I meet . . . . the effect upon me of my early life . . . . of the ward
        and city I live in . . . . of the nation,
    The latest news . . . . discoveries, inventions, societies . . . . authors old
60   and new,
    My dinner, dress, associates, looks, business, compliments, dues,
    The real or fancied indifference of some man or woman I love,
    The sickness of one of my folks—or of myself . . . . or ill-doing . . . . or
        loss or lack of money . . . . or depressions or exaltations,
    They come to me days and nights and go from me again,
65 But they are not the Me myself.

    Apart from the pulling and hauling stands what I am,
    Stands amused, complacent, compassionating, idle, unitary,
    Looks down, is erect, bends an arm on an impalpable certain rest,
    Looks with its sidecurved head curious what will come next,
70 Both in and out of the game, and watching and wondering at it.

    Backward I see in my own days where I sweated through fog with
        linguists and contenders,
    I have no mockings or arguments . . . . I witness and wait.

    I believe in you my soul . . . . the other I am must not abase itself
        to you,
    And you must not be abased to the other.

75 Loafe with me on the grass . . . . loose the stop from your throat,
    Not words, not music or rhyme I want . . . . not custom or lecture, not
        even the best,
    Only the lull I like, the hum of your valved voice.

I mind how we lay in June, such a transparent summer morning;
You settled your head athwart my hips and gently turned over upon me.
And parted the shirt from my bosom-bone, and plunged your tongue
    to my barestript heart, 80
And reached till you felt my beard, and reached till you held my feet.

Swiftly arose and spread around me the peace and joy and knowledge
    that pass all the art and argument of the earth;
And I know that the hand of God is the elderhand of my own,
And I know that the spirit of God is the eldest brother of my own,
And that all the men ever born are also my brothers . . . . and the
    women my sisters and lovers, 85
And that a kelson of the creation is love;
And limitless are leaves stiff or drooping in the fields,
And brown ants in the little wells beneath them,
And mossy scabs of the wormfence, and heaped stones, and elder and
    mullen and pokeweed.

A child said, What is the grass? fetching it to me with full hands; 90
How could I answer the child? . . . . I do not know what it is any more
    than he.

I guess it must be the flag of my disposition, out of hopeful green stuff
    woven.

Or I guess it is the handkerchief of the Lord,
A scented gift and remembrancer designedly dropped,
Bearing the owner's name someway in the corners, that we may see
    and remark, and say Whose? 95

Or I guess the grass is itself a child . . . . the produced babe of the
    vegetation.

Or I guess it is a uniform hieroglyphic,
And it means, Sprouting alike in broad zones and narrow zones,

Growing among black folks as among white,
Kanuck, Tuckahoe, Congressman, Cuff, I give them the same, I receive
100   them the same.

And now it seems to me the beautiful uncut hair of graves.

Tenderly will I use you curling grass,
It may be you transpire from the breasts of young men,
It may be if I had known them I would have loved them;
It may be you are from old people and from women, and from
105   offspring taken soon out of their mothers' laps,
And here you are the mothers' laps.

This grass is very dark to be from the white heads of old mothers,
Darker than the colorless beards of old men,
Dark to come from under the faint red roofs of mouths.

110 O I perceive after all so many uttering tongues!
And I perceive they do not come from the roofs of mouths for
       nothing.

I wish I could translate the hints about the dead young men and
       women,
And the hints about old men and mothers, and the offspring taken
       soon out of their laps.

What do you think has become of the young and old men?
115 And what do you think has become of the women and children?

They are alive and well somewhere;
The smallest sprout shows there is really no death,
And if ever there was it led forward life, and does not wait at the end to
       arrest it,
And ceased the moment life appeared.

All goes onward and outward . . . . and nothing collapses,   120
And to die is different from what any one supposed, and luckier.

Has any one supposed it lucky to be born?
I hasten to inform him or her it is just as lucky to die, and I
 know it.

I pass death with the dying, and birth with the new-washed babe . . . .
 and am not contained between my hat and boots,
And peruse manifold objects, no two alike, and every one good,   125
The earth good, and the stars good, and their adjuncts all good.

I am not an earth nor an adjunct of an earth,
I am the mate and companion of people, all just as immortal and
 fathomless as myself;
They do not know how immortal, but I know.

Every kind for itself and its own . . . . for me mine male and female,   130
For me all that have been boys and that love women,
For me the man that is proud and feels how it stings to be slighted,
For me the sweetheart and the old maid . . . . for me mothers and the
 mothers of mothers,
For me lips that have smiled, eyes that have shed tears,
For me children and the begetters of children.   135

Who need be afraid of the merge?
Undrape . . . . you are not guilty to me, nor stale nor discarded,
I see through the broadcloth and gingham whether or no,
And am around, tenacious, acquisitive, tireless . . . . and can never be
 shaken away.

The little one sleeps in its cradle,   140
I lift the gauze and look a long time, and silently brush away flies with
 my hand.

The youngster and the redfaced girl turn aside up the bushy hill,
I peeringly view them from the top.

The suicide sprawls on the bloody floor of the bedroom,
145 It is so .... I witnessed the corpse .... there the pistol had fallen.

The blab of the pave .... the tires of carts and sluff of bootsoles and
    talk of the promenaders,
The heavy omnibus, the driver with his interrogating thumb, the clank
    of the shod horses on the granite floor,
The carnival of sleighs, the clinking and shouted jokes and pelts of
    snowballs;
The hurrahs for popular favorites .... the fury of roused mobs,
The flap of the curtained litter—the sick man inside, borne to the
150   hospital,
The meeting of enemies, the sudden oath, the blows and fall,
The excited crowd—the policeman with his star quickly working his
    passage to the centre of the crowd;
The impassive stones that receive and return so many echoes,
The souls moving along .... are they invisible while the least atom of
    the stones is visible?
What groans of overfed or half-starved who fall on the flags sunstruck
155   or in fits,
What exclamations of women taken suddenly, who hurry home and
    give birth to babes,
What living and buried speech is always vibrating here .... what howls
    restrained by decorum,
Arrests of criminals, slights, adulterous offers made, acceptances,
    rejections with convex lips,
I mind them or the resonance of them .... I come again and again.

160 The big doors of the country-barn stand open and ready,
The dried grass of the harvest-time loads the slow-drawn wagon,
The clear light plays on the brown gray and green intertinged,
The armfuls are packed to the sagging mow:
I am there .... I help .... I came stretched atop of the load,

I felt its soft jolts . . . . one leg reclined on the other,   165
I jump from the crossbeams, and seize the clover and timothy,
And roll head over heels, and tangle my hair full of wisps.

Alone far in the wilds and mountains I hunt,
Wandering amazed at my own lightness and glee,
In the late afternoon choosing a safe spot to pass the night,   170
Kindling a fire and broiling the freshkilled game,
Soundly falling asleep on the gathered leaves, my dog and gun by my
      side.

The Yankee clipper is under her three skysails . . . . she cuts the sparkle
      and scud,
My eyes settle the land . . . . I bend at her prow or shout joyously from
      the deck.

The boatmen and clamdiggers arose early and stopped for me,   175
I tucked my trowser-ends in my boots and went and had a good time,
You should have been with us that day round the chowder-kettle.

I saw the marriage of the trapper in the open air in the far-west . . . .
      the bride was a red girl,
Her father and his friends sat near by crosslegged and dumbly
      smoking . . . . they had moccasins to their feet and large thick
      blankets hanging from their shoulders;
On a bank lounged the trapper . . . . he was dressed mostly in skins . . . .
      his luxuriant beard and curls protected his neck,   180
One hand rested on his rifle . . . . the other hand held firmly the wrist
      of the red girl.
She had long eyelashes . . . . her head was bare . . . . her coarse straight
      locks descended upon her voluptuous limbs and reached to her
      feet.

The runaway slave came to my house and stopped outside,
I heard his motions crackling the twigs of the woodpile,

Through the swung half-door of the kitchen I saw him limpsey and
185   weak,
    And went where he sat on a log, and led him in and assured him,
    And brought water and filled a tub for his sweated body and bruised
        feet,
    And gave him a room that entered from my own, and gave him some
        coarse clean clothes,
    And remember perfectly well his revolving eyes and his awkwardness,
190 And remember putting plasters on the galls of his neck and ankles;
    He staid with me a week before he was recuperated and passed north,
    I had him sit next me at table . . . . my firelock leaned in the corner.

    Twenty-eight young men bathe by the shore,
    Twenty-eight young men, and all so friendly,
195 Twenty-eight years of womanly life, and all so lonesome.

    She owns the fine house by the rise of the bank,
    She hides handsome and richly drest aft the blinds of the window.

    Which of the young men does she like the best?
    Ah the homeliest of them is beautiful to her.

200 Where are you off to, lady? for I see you,
    You splash in the water there, yet stay stock still in your room.

    Dancing and laughing along the beach came the twenty-ninth bather,
    The rest did not see her, but she saw them and loved them.

    The beards of the young men glistened with wet, it ran from their long
        hair,
205 Little streams passed all over their bodies.

    An unseen hand also passed over their bodies,
    It descended tremblingly from their temples and ribs.

The young men float on their backs, their white bellies swell to the
    sun . . . . they do not ask who seizes fast to them,
They do not know who puffs and declines with pendant and bending arch,
They do not think whom they souse with spray.   210

The butcher-boy puts off his killing-clothes, or sharpens his knife at
    the stall in the market,
I loiter enjoying his repartee and his shuffle and breakdown.

Blacksmiths with grimed and hairy chests environ the anvil,
Each has his main-sledge . . . . they are all out . . . . there is a great heat
    in the fire.

From the cinder-strewed threshold I follow their movements,   215
The lithe sheer of their waists plays even with their massive arms,
Overhand the hammers roll—overhand so slow—overhand so sure,
They do not hasten, each man hits in his place.

The negro holds firmly the reins of his four horses . . . . the block swags
    underneath on its tied-over chain,
The negro that drives the huge dray of the stoneyard . . . . steady and
    tall he stands poised on one leg on the stringpiece,   220
His blue shirt exposes his ample neck and breast and loosens over his
    hipband,
His glance is calm and commanding . . . . he tosses the slouch of his hat
    away from his forehead,
The sun falls on his crispy hair and moustache . . . . falls on the black of
    his polish'd and perfect limbs.

I behold the picturesque giant and love him . . . . and I do not stop there,
I go with the team also.   225

In me the caresser of life wherever moving . . . . backward as well as
    forward slueing,
To niches aside and junior bending.

Oxen that rattle the yoke or halt in the shade, what is that you express
    in your eyes?
It seems to me more than all the print I have read in my life.

My tread scares the wood-drake and wood-duck on my distant and
230   daylong ramble,
They rise together, they slowly circle around.
. . . . I believe in those winged purposes,
And acknowledge the red yellow and white playing within me,
And consider the green and violet and the tufted crown intentional;
And do not call the tortoise unworthy because she is not something
235   else,
And the mockingbird in the swamp never studied the gamut, yet trills
    pretty well to me,
And the look of the bay mare shames silliness out of me.

The wild gander leads his flock through the cool night,
Ya-honk! he says, and sounds it down to me like an invitation;
240 The pert may suppose it meaningless, but I listen closer,
I find its purpose and place up there toward the November sky.

The sharphoofed moose of the north, the cat on the housesill, the
    chickadee, the prairie-dog,
The litter of the grunting sow as they tug at her teats,
The brood of the turkeyhen, and she with her halfspread wings,
245 I see in them and myself the same old law.

The press of my foot to the earth springs a hundred affections,
They scorn the best I can do to relate them.

I am enamoured of growing outdoors,
Of men that live among cattle or taste of the ocean or woods,
Of the builders and steerers of ships, of the wielders of axes and mauls,
250   of the drivers of horses,
I can eat and sleep with them week in and week out.

What is commonest and cheapest and nearest and easiest is Me,
Me going in for my chances, spending for vast returns,
Adorning myself to bestow myself on the first that will take me,
Not asking the sky to come down to my goodwill,   255
Scattering it freely forever.

The pure contralto sings in the organloft,
The carpenter dresses his plank . . . . the tongue of his foreplane
    whistles its wild ascending lisp,
The married and unmarried children ride home to their thanksgiving
    dinner,
The pilot seizes the king-pin, he heaves down with a strong arm,   260
The mate stands braced in the whaleboat, lance and harpoon are ready,
The duck-shooter walks by silent and cautious stretches,
The deacons are ordained with crossed hands at the altar,
The spinning-girl retreats and advances to the hum of the big wheel,
The farmer stops by the bars of a Sunday and looks at the oats
    and rye,   265
The lunatic is carried at last to the asylum a confirmed case,
He will never sleep any more as he did in the cot in his mother's
    bedroom;
The jour printer with gray head and gaunt jaws works at his case,
He turns his quid of tobacco, his eyes get blurred with the manuscript;
The malformed limbs are tied to the anatomist's table,   270
What is removed drops horribly in a pail;
The quadroon girl is sold at the stand . . . . the drunkard nods by the
    barroom stove,
The machinist rolls up his sleeves . . . . the policeman travels his
    beat . . . . the gate-keeper marks who pass,
The young fellow drives the express-wagon . . . . I love him though I do
    not know him;
The half-breed straps on his light boots to compete in the race,   275
The western turkey-shooting draws old and young . . . . some lean on
    their rifles, some sit on logs,
Out from the crowd steps the marksman and takes his position and
    levels his piece;

The groups of newly-come immigrants cover the wharf or levee,

The woollypates hoe in the sugarfield, the overseer views them from
his saddle;

The bugle calls in the ballroom, the gentlemen run for their partners,
280   the dancers bow to each other;

The youth lies awake in the cedar-roofed garret and harks to the
musical rain,

The Wolverine sets traps on the creek that helps fill the Huron,

The reformer ascends the platform, he spouts with his mouth and nose,

The company returns from its excursion, the darkey brings up the rear
and bears the well-riddled target,

The squaw wrapt in her yellow-hemmed cloth is offering moccasins
285   and beadbags for sale,

The connoisseur peers along the exhibition-gallery with halfshut eyes
bent sideways,

The deckhands make fast the steamboat, the plank is thrown for the
shoregoing passengers,

The young sister holds out the skein, the elder sister winds it off in a
ball and stops now and then for the knots,

The one-year wife is recovering and happy, a week ago she bore her
first child,

The cleanhaired Yankee girl works with her sewing-machine or in the
290   factory or mill,

The nine months' gone is in the parturition chamber, her faintness and
pains are advancing;

The pavingman leans on his twohanded rammer—the reporter's lead
flies swiftly over the notebook—the signpainter is lettering with red
and gold,

The canal-boy trots on the towpath—the bookkeeper counts at his
desk—the shoemaker waxes his thread,

The conductor beats time for the band and all the performers follow
him,

295 The child is baptised—the convert is making the first professions,

The regatta is spread on the bay . . . . how the white sails sparkle!

The drover watches his drove, he sings out to them that would stray,

The pedlar sweats with his pack on his back—the purchaser higgles
about the odd cent,

The camera and plate are prepared, the lady must sit for her
    daguerreotype,
The bride unrumples her white dress, the minutehand of the clock
    moves slowly,   300
The opium eater reclines with rigid head and just-opened lips,
The prostitute draggles her shawl, her bonnet bobs on her tipsy and
    pimpled neck,
The crowd laugh at her blackguard oaths, the men jeer and wink to
    each other,
(Miserable! I do not laugh at your oaths nor jeer you,)
The President holds a cabinet council, he is surrounded by the great
    secretaries,   305
On the piazza walk five friendly matrons with twined arms;
The crew of the fish-smack pack repeated layers of halibut in the hold,
The Missourian crosses the plains toting his wares and his cattle,
The fare-collector goes through the train—he gives notice by the
    jingling of loose change,
The floormen are laying the floor—the tinners are tinning the
    roof—the masons are calling for mortar,   310
In single file each shouldering his hod pass onward the laborers;
Seasons pursuing each other the indescribable crowd is gathered . . . . it
    is the Fourth of July . . . . what salutes of cannon and small arms!
Seasons pursuing each other the plougher ploughs and the mower
    mows and the wintergrain falls in the ground;
Off on the lakes the pikefisher watches and waits by the hole in the
    frozen surface,
The stumps stand thick round the clearing, the squatter strikes deep
    with his axe,   315
The flatboatmen make fast toward dusk near the cottonwood or
    pekantrees,
The coon-seekers go now through the regions of the Red river, or
    through those drained by the Tennessee, or through those of the
    Arkansas,
The torches shine in the dark that hangs on the Chattahoochee or
    Altamahaw;
Patriarchs sit at supper with sons and grandsons and great grandsons
    around them,

In walls of adobe in canvass tents, rest hunters and trappers after their
320   day's sport.
The city sleeps and the country sleeps,
The living sleep for their time . . . . the dead sleep for their time,
The old husband sleeps by his wife and the young husband sleeps by
his wife;
And these one and all tend inward to me, and I tend outward to them,
325   And such as it is to be of these more or less I am.

I am of old and young, of the foolish as much as the wise,
Regardless of others, ever regardful of others,
Maternal as well as paternal, a child as well as a man,
Stuffed with the stuff that is coarse, and stuffed with the stuff that is
fine,
One of the great nation, the nation of many nations—the smallest the
330   same and the largest the same,
A southerner soon as a northerner, a planter nonchalant and
hospitable,
A Yankee bound my own way . . . . ready for trade . . . . my joints the
limberest joints on earth and the sternest joints on earth,
A Kentuckian walking the vale of the Elkhorn in my deerskin
leggings,
A boatman over the lakes or bays or along coasts . . . . a Hoosier, a
Badger, a Buckeye,
335   A Louisianian or Georgian, a poke-easy from sandhills and pines,
At home on Canadian snowshoes or up in the bush, or with fishermen
off New-foundland,
At home in the fleet of iceboats, sailing with the rest and tacking,
At home on the hills of Vermont or in the woods of Maine or the
Texan ranch,
Comrade of Californians . . . . comrade of free northwesterners, loving
their big proportions,
Comrade of raftsmen and coalmen—comrade of all who shake hands
340   and welcome to drink and meat;
A learner with the simplest, a teacher of the thoughtfulest,
A novice beginning experient of myriads of seasons,

Of every hue and trade and rank, of every caste and religion,
Not merely of the New World but of Africa Europe or Asia . . . .
    a wandering savage,
A farmer, mechanic, or artist . . . . a gentleman, sailor, lover or
    quaker,   345
A prisoner, fancy-man, rowdy, lawyer, physician or priest.

I resist anything better than my own diversity,
And breathe the air and leave plenty after me,
And am not stuck up, and am in my place.

The moth and the fisheggs are in their place,   350
The suns I see and the suns I cannot see are in their place,
The palpable is in its place and the impalpable is in its place.

These are the thoughts of all men in all ages and lands, they are not
    original with me,
If they are not yours as much as mine they are nothing or next to
    nothing,
If they do not enclose everything they are next to nothing,   355
If they are not the riddle and the untying of the riddle they are
    nothing,
If they are not just as close as they are distant they are nothing.

This is the grass that grows wherever the land is and the water is,
This is the common air that bathes the globe.

This is the breath of laws and songs and behaviour,   360
This is the tasteless water of souls . . . . this is the true sustenance,
It is for the illiterate . . . . it is for the judges of the supreme court . . . . it
    is for the federal capitol and the state capitols,
It is for the admirable communes of literary men and composers and
    singers and lecturers and engineers and savans,
It is for the endless races of working people and farmers and seamen.

This is the trill of a thousand clear cornets and scream of the octave
365   flute and strike of triangles.

I play not a march for victors only . . . . I play great marches for
    conquered and slain persons.

Have you heard that it was good to gain the day?
I also say it is good to fall . . . . battles are lost in the same spirit in
    which they are won.

I sound triumphal drums for the dead . . . . I fling through my
    embouchures the loudest and gayest music to them,
Vivas to those who have failed, and to those whose war-vessels sank in
370   the sea, and those themselves who sank in the sea,
And to all generals that lost engagements, and all overcome heroes, and
    the number-less unknown heroes equal to the greatest heroes known.

This is the meal pleasantly set . . . . this is the meat and drink for
    natural hunger,
It is for the wicked just the same as the righteous . . . . I make
    appointments with all,
I will not have a single person slighted or left away,
The keptwoman and sponger and thief are hereby invited . . . . the
375   heavy-lipped slave is invited . . . . the venerealee is invited,
There shall be no difference between them and the rest.

This is the press of a bashful hand . . . . this is the float and odor of hair,
This is the touch of my lips to yours . . . . this is the murmur of yearning,
This is the far-off depth and height reflecting my own face,
380 This is the thoughtful merge of myself and the outlet again.

Do you guess I have some intricate purpose?
Well I have . . . . for the April rain has, and the mica on the side of a
    rock has.

Do you take it I would astonish?
Does the daylight astonish? or the early redstart twittering through the
    woods?
Do I astonish more than they?   385

This hour I tell things in confidence,
I might not tell everybody but I will tell you.

Who goes there! hankering, gross, mystical, nude?
How is it I extract strength from the beef I eat?

What is a man anyhow? What am I? and what are you?   390
All I mark as my own you shall offset it with your own,
Else it were time lost listening to me.

I do not snivel that snivel the world over,
That months are vacuums and the ground but wallow and filth,
That life is a suck and a sell, and nothing remains at the end but
    threadbare crape and tears.   395

Whimpering and truckling fold with powders for invalids . . . .
    conformity goes to the fourth-removed,
I cock my hat as I please indoors or out.

Shall I pray? Shall I venerate and be ceremonious?

I have pried through the strata and analyzed to a hair,
And counselled with doctors and calculated close and found no
    sweeter fat than sticks to my own bones.   400

In all people I see myself, none more and not one a barleycorn
    less,
And the good or bad I say of myself I say of them.

And I know I am solid and sound,
To me the converging objects of the universe perpetually flow,
405 All are written to me, and I must get what the writing means.

And I know I am deathless,
I know this orbit of mine cannot be swept by a carpenter's compass,
I know I shall not pass like a child's carlacue cut with a burnt stick at
     night.

I know I am august,
410 I do not trouble my spirit to vindicate itself or be understood,
I see that the elementary laws never apologize,
I reckon I behave no prouder than the level I plant my house by
     after all.

I exist as I am, that is enough,
If no other in the world be aware I sit content,
415 And if each and all be aware I sit content.

One world is aware, and by far the largest to me, and that is myself,
And whether I come to my own today or in ten thousand or ten
     million years,
I can cheerfully take it now, or with equal cheerfulness I can wait.

My foothold is tenoned and mortised in granite,
420 I laugh at what you call dissolution,
And I know the amplitude of time.

I am the poet of the body,
And I am the poet of the soul.

The pleasures of heaven are with me, and the pains of hell are with me,
The first I graft and increase upon myself . . . . the latter I translate into
425   a new tongue.

I am the poet of the woman the same as the man,
And I say it is as great to be a woman as to be a man,
And I say there is nothing greater than the mother of men.

I chant a new chant of dilation or pride,
We have had ducking and deprecating about enough,   430
I show that size is only developement.

Have you outstript the rest? Are you the President?
It is a trifle . . . . they will more than arrive there every one, and still
    pass on.

I am he that walks with the tender and growing night;
I call to the earth and sea half-held by the night.   435

Press close barebosomed night! Press close magnetic nourishing
    night!
Night of south winds! Night of the large few stars!
Still nodding night! Mad naked summer night!

Smile O voluptuous coolbreathed earth!
Earth of the slumbering and liquid trees!   440
Earth of departed sunset! Earth of the mountains misty-topt!
Earth of the vitreous pour of the full moon just tinged with blue!
Earth of shine and dark mottling the tide of the river!
Earth of the limpid gray of clouds brighter and clearer for my sake!
Far-swooping elbowed earth! Rich apple-blossomed earth!   445
Smile, for your lover comes!

Prodigal! you have given me love! . . . . therefore I to you give love!
O unspeakable passionate love!

Thruster holding me tight and that I hold tight!
We hurt each other as the bridegroom and the bride hurt each other.   450

You sea! I resign myself to you also . . . . I guess what you mean,
I behold from the beach your crooked inviting fingers,
I believe you refuse to go back without feeling of me;
We must have a turn together . . . . I undress . . . . hurry me out of sight
    of the land,
455 Cushion me soft . . . . rock me in billowy drowse,
Dash me with amorous wet . . . . I can repay you.

Sea of stretched ground-swells!
Sea breathing broad and convulsive breaths!
Sea of the brine of life! Sea of unshovelled and always-ready
    graves!
460 Howler and scooper of storms! Capricious and dainty sea!
I am integral with you . . . . I too am of one phase and of all phases.

Partaker of influx and efflux . . . . extoler of hate and conciliation,
Extoler of amies and those that sleep in each others' arms.

I am he attesting sympathy;
Shall I make my list of things in the house and skip the house that
465   supports them?

I am the poet of commonsense and of the demonstrable and of
    immortality;
And am not the poet of goodness only . . . . I do not decline to be the
    poet of wickedness also.

Washes and razors for foofoos . . . . for me freckles and a bristling
    beard.

What blurt is it about virtue and about vice?
470 Evil propels me, and reform of evil propels me . . . . I stand indifferent,
My gait is no faultfinder's or rejecter's gait,
I moisten the roots of all that has grown.

Did you fear some scrofula out of the unflagging pregnancy?
Did you guess the celestial laws are yet to be worked over and rectified?

I step up to say that what we do is right and what we affirm is right . . . .
    and some is only the ore of right,   475
Witnesses of us . . . . one side a balance and the antipodal side a
    balance,
Soft doctrine as steady help as stable doctrine,
Thoughts and deeds of the present our rouse and early start.

This minute that comes to me over the past decillions,
There is no better than it and now.   480

What behaved well in the past or behaves well today is not such a
    wonder,
The wonder is always and always how there can be a mean man or an
    infidel.

Endless unfolding of words of ages!
And mine a word of the modern . . . . a word en masse.

A word of the faith that never balks,   485
One time as good as another time . . . . here or henceforward it is all
    the same to me.

A word of reality . . . . materialism first and last imbueing.

Hurrah for positive science! Long live exact demonstration!
Fetch stonecrop and mix it with cedar and branches of lilac;
This is the lexicographer or chemist . . . . this made a grammar of the
    old cartouches,   490
These mariners put the ship through dangerous unknown seas,
This is the geologist, and this works with the scalpel, and this is a
    mathematician.

Gentlemen I receive you, and attach and clasp hands with you,
The facts are useful and real . . . . they are not my dwelling . . . . I enter
    by them to an area of the dwelling.

I am less the reminder of property or qualities, and more the reminder
495   of life,
And go on the square for my own sake and for others' sakes,
And make short account of neuters and geldings, and favor men and
    women fully equipped,
And beat the gong of revolt, and stop with fugitives and them that plot
    and conspire.

Walt Whitman, an American, one of the roughs, a kosmos,
500 Disorderly fleshy and sensual . . . . eating drinking and breeding,
No sentimentalist . . . . no stander above men and women or apart from
    them . . . . no more modest than immodest.

Unscrew the locks from the doors!
Unscrew the doors themselves from their jambs!

Whoever degrades another degrades me . . . . and whatever is done or
    said returns at last to me,
505 And whatever I do or say I also return.

Through me the afflatus surging and surging . . . . through me the
    current and index.

I speak the password primeval . . . . I give the sign of democracy;
By God! I will accept nothing which all cannot have their counterpart
    of on the same terms.

Through me many long dumb voices,
510 Voices of the interminable generations of slaves,
Voices of prostitutes and of deformed persons,

Voices of the diseased and despairing, and of thieves and dwarfs,
Voices of cycles of preparation and accretion,
And of the threads that connect the stars—and of wombs, and of the
    fatherstuff,
And of the rights of them the others are down upon,   515
Of the trivial and flat and foolish and despised,
Of fog in the air and beetles rolling balls of dung.

Through me forbidden voices,
Voices of sexes and lusts . . . . voices veiled, and I remove the veil,
Voices indecent by me clarified and transfigured.   520

I do not press my finger across my mouth,
I keep as delicate around the bowels as around the head and heart,
Copulation is no more rank to me than death is.

I believe in the flesh and the appetites,
Seeing hearing and feeling are miracles, and each part and tag of me is
    a miracle.   525

Divine am I inside and out, and I make holy whatever I touch or am
    touched from;
The scent of these arm-pits is aroma finer than prayer,
This head is more than churches or bibles or creeds.

If I worship any particular thing it shall be some of the spread of my
    body;
Translucent mould of me it shall be you,   530
Shaded ledges and rests, firm masculine coulter, it shall be you,
Whatever goes to the tilth of me it shall be you,
You my rich blood, your milky stream pale strippings of my life;
Breast that presses against other breasts it shall be you,
My brain it shall be your occult convolutions,   535
Root of washed sweet-flag, timorous pond-snipe, nest of guarded
    duplicate eggs, it shall be you,

Mixed tussled hay of head and beard and brawn it shall be you,
Trickling sap of maple, fibre of manly wheat, it shall be you;
Sun so generous it shall be you,
540 Vapors lighting and shading my face it shall be you,
You sweaty brooks and dews it shall be you,
Winds whose soft-tickling genitals rub against me it shall be you,
Broad muscular fields, branches of liveoak, loving lounger in my
   winding paths, it shall be you,
Hands I have taken, face I have kissed, mortal I have ever touched, it
   shall be you.

545 I dote on myself . . . . there is that lot of me, and all so luscious,
Each moment and whatever happens thrills me with joy.

I cannot tell how my ankles bend . . . . nor whence the cause of my
   faintest wish,
Nor the cause of the friendship I emit . . . . nor the cause of the
   friendship I take again.

To walk up my stoop is unaccountable . . . . I pause to consider if it
   really be,
550 That I eat and drink is spectacle enough for the great authors and schools,
A morning-glory at my window satisfies me more than the
   metaphysics of books.

To behold the daybreak!
The little light fades the immense and diaphanous shadows,
The air tastes good to my palate.

Hefts of the moving world at innocent gambols, silently rising, freshly
555   exuding,
Scooting obliquely high and low.

Something I cannot see puts upward libidinous prongs,
Seas of bright juice suffuse heaven.

The earth by the sky staid with . . . . the daily close of their junction,
The heaved challenge from the east that moment over my head,   560
The mocking taunt, See then whether you shall be master!

Dazzling and tremendous how quick the sunrise would kill me,
If I could not now and always send sunrise out of me.

We also ascend dazzling and tremendous as the sun,
We found our own my soul in the calm and cool of the daybreak.   565

My voice goes after what my eyes cannot reach,
With the twirl of my tongue I encompass worlds and volumes of
    worlds.

Speech is the twin of my vision . . . . it is unequal to measure itself.

It provokes me forever,
It says sarcastically, Walt, you understand enough . . . . why don't you
    let it out then?   570

Come now I will not be tantalized . . . . you conceive too much of
    articulation.

Do you not know how the buds beneath are folded?
Waiting in gloom protected by frost,
The dirt receding before my prophetical screams,
I underlying causes to balance them at last,   575
My knowledge my live parts . . . . it keeping tally with the meaning of
    things,
Happiness . . . . which whoever hears me let him or her set out in search
    of this day.

My final merit I refuse you . . . . I refuse putting from me the best
    I am.

Encompass worlds but never try to encompass me,
580 I crowd your noisiest talk by looking toward you.

Writing and talk do not prove me,
I carry the plenum of proof and every thing else in my face,
With the hush of my lips I confound the topmost skeptic.

I think I will do nothing for a long time but listen,
And accrue what I hear into myself . . . . and let sounds contribute
585   toward me.

I hear the bravuras of birds . . . . the bustle of growing wheat . . . . gossip
of flames . . . . clack of sticks cooking my meals.

I hear the sound of the human voice . . . . a sound I love,
I hear all sounds as they are tuned to their uses . . . . sounds of the city
and sounds out of the city . . . . sounds of the day and night;
Talkative young ones to those that like them . . . . the recitative of
fish-pedlars and fruit-pedlars . . . . the loud laugh of workpeople at
their meals,
The angry base of disjointed friendship . . . . the faint tones of the
590   sick,
The judge with hands tight to the desk, his shaky lips pronouncing a
death-sentence,
The heave'e'yo of stevedores unlading ships by the wharves . . . . the
refrain of the anchor-lifters;

The ring of alarm-bells . . . . the cry of fire . . . . the whirr of swift-
streaking engines and hose-carts with premonitory tinkles and
colored lights,
The steam-whistle . . . . the solid roll of the train of approaching
cars;
595 The slow-march played at night at the head of the association,
They go to guard some corpse . . . . the flag-tops are draped with black
muslin.

I hear the violincello or man's heart's complaint,
And hear the keyed cornet or else the echo of sunset.

I hear the chorus . . . . it is a grand-opera . . . . this indeed is music!

A tenor large and fresh as the creation fills me,   600
The orbic flex of his mouth is pouring and filling me full.

I hear the trained soprano . . . . she convulses me like the climax of my
  love-grip;
The orchestra whirls me wider than Uranus flies,
It wrenches unnamable ardors from my breast,
It throbs me to gulps of the farthest down horror,   605
It sails me . . . . I dab with bare feet . . . . they are licked by the indolent
  waves,
I am exposed . . . . cut by bitter and poisoned hail,
Steeped amid honeyed morphine . . . . my windpipe squeezed in the
  fakes of death,
Let up again to feel the puzzle of puzzles,
And that we call Being.   610

To be in any form, what is that?
If nothing lay more developed the quahaug and its callous shell were
  enough.

Mine is no callous shell,
I have instant conductors all over me whether I pass or stop,
They seize every object and lead it harmlessly through me.   615

I merely stir, press, feel with my fingers, and am happy,
To touch my person to some one else's is about as much as I can stand.

Is this then a touch? . . . . quivering me to a new identity,
Flames and ether making a rush for my veins,

620 Treacherous tip of me reaching and crowding to help them,
   My flesh and blood playing out lightning, to strike what is hardly
      different from myself,
   On all sides prurient provokers stiffening my limbs,
   Straining the udder of my heart for its withheld drip,
   Behaving licentious toward me, taking no denial,
625 Depriving me of my best as for a purpose,
   Unbuttoning my clothes and holding me by the bare waist,
   Deluding my confusion with the calm of the sunlight and pasture
      fields,

   Immodestly sliding the fellow-senses away,
   They bribed to swap off with touch, and go and graze at the edges
      of me,
630 No consideration, no regard for my draining strength or my anger,
   Fetching the rest of the herd around to enjoy them awhile,
   Then all uniting to stand on a headland and worry me.

   The sentries desert every other part of me,
   They have left me helpless to a red marauder,
635 They all come to the headland to witness and assist against me.

   I am given up by traitors;
   I talk wildly . . . . I have lost my wits . . . . I and nobody else am the
      greatest traitor,
   I went myself first to the headland . . . . my own hands carried me
      there.

   You villain touch! what are you doing? . . . . my breath is tight in its
      throat;
640 Unclench your floodgates! you are too much for me.

   Blind loving wrestling touch! Sheathed hooded sharptoothed
      touch!
   Did it make you ache so leaving me?

Parting tracked by arriving . . . . perpetual payment of the perpetual
　　loan,
Rich showering rain, and recompense richer afterward.

Sprouts take and accumulate . . . . stand by the curb prolific and vital,　　645
Landscapes projected masculine full-sized and golden.

All truths wait in all things,
They neither hasten their own delivery nor resist it,
They do not need the obstetric forceps of the surgeon,
The insignificant is as big to me as any,　　650
What is less or more than a touch?

Logic and sermons never convince,
The damp of the night drives deeper into my soul.

Only what proves itself to every man and woman is so,
Only what nobody denies is so.　　655

A minute and a drop of me settle my brain;
I believe the soggy clods shall become lovers and lamps,
And a compend of compends is the meat of a man or woman,
And a summit and flower there is the feeling they have for each
　　other,
And they are to branch boundlessly out of that lesson until it becomes
　　omnific,　　660
And until every one shall delight us, and we them.

I believe a leaf of grass is no less than the journeywork of the stars,
And the pismire is equally perfect, and a grain of sand, and the egg of
　　the wren,
And the tree-toad is a chef-d'ouvre for the highest,
And the running blackberry would adorn the parlors of heaven,　　665
And the narrowest hinge in my hand puts to scorn all machinery,
And the cow crunching with depressed head surpasses any statue,

And a mouse is miracle enough to stagger sextillions of infidels,
And I could come every afternoon of my life to look at the farmer's girl
  boiling her iron tea-kettle and baking shortcake.

I find I incorporate gneiss and coal and long-threaded moss and fruits
670   and grains and esculent roots,
And am stucco'd with quadrupeds and birds all over,
And have distanced what is behind me for good reasons,
And call any thing close again when I desire it.

In vain the speeding or shyness,
In vain the plutonic rocks send their old heat against my
675   approach,
In vain the mastadon retreats beneath its own powdered bones,
In vain objects stand leagues off and assume manifold shapes,
In vain the ocean settling in hollows and the great monsters lying
  low,
In vain the buzzard houses herself with the sky,
680 In vain the snake slides through the creepers and logs,
In vain the elk takes to the inner passes of the woods,
In vain the razorbilled auk sails far north to Labrador,
I follow quickly . . . . I ascend to the nest in the fissure of the cliff.

I think I could turn and live awhile with the animals . . . . they are so
  placid and self-contained,
685 I stand and look at them sometimes half the day long.

They do not sweat and whine about their condition,
They do not lie awake in the dark and weep for their sins,
They do not make me sick discussing their duty to God,
Not one is dissatisfied . . . . not one is demented with the mania of
  owning things,
Not one kneels to another nor to his kind that lived thousands of years
690   ago,
Not one is respectable or industrious over the whole earth.

So they show their relations to me and I accept them;
They bring me tokens of myself . . . . they evince them plainly in their
    possession.

I do not know where they got those tokens,
I must have passed that way untold times ago and negligently dropt them, 695
Myself moving forward then and now and forever,
Gathering and showing more always and with velocity,
Infinite and omnigenous and the like of these among them;
Not too exclusive toward the reachers of my remembrancers,
Picking out here one that shall be my amie,   700
Choosing to go with him on brotherly terms.

A gigantic beauty of a stallion, fresh and responsive to my caresses,
Head high in the forehead and wide between the ears,
Limbs glossy and supple, tail dusting the ground,
Eyes well apart and full of sparkling wickedness . . . . ears finely cut
    and flexibly moving.   705

His nostrils dilate . . . . my heels embrace him . . . . his well built limbs
    tremble with pleasure . . . . we speed around and return.

I but use you a moment and then I resign you stallion . . . . and do not
    need your paces, and outgallop them,
And myself as I stand or sit pass faster than you.

Swift wind! Space! My Soul! Now I know it is true what I guessed at;
What I guessed when I loafed on the grass,   710
What I guessed while I lay alone in my bed . . . . and again as I walked
    the beach under the paling stars of the morning.

My ties and ballasts leave me . . . . I travel . . . . I sail . . . . my elbows rest
    in the sea-gaps,
I skirt the sierras . . . . my palms cover continents,
I am afoot with my vision.

By the city's quadrangular houses . . . . in log-huts, or camping with
715   lumbermen,
Along the ruts of the turnpike . . . . along the dry gulch and rivulet
bed,
Hoeing my onion-patch, and rows of carrots and parsnips . . . . crossing
savannas . . . . trailing in forests,
Prospecting . . . . gold-digging . . . . girdling the trees of a new
purchase,
Scorched ankle-deep by the hot sand . . . . hauling my boat down the
shallow river;
Where the panther walks to and fro on a limb overhead . . . . where the
720   buck turns furiously at the hunter,
Where the rattlesnake suns his flabby length on a rock . . . . where the
otter is feeding on fish,
Where the alligator in his tough pimples sleeps by the bayou,
Where the black bear is searching for roots or honey . . . . where the
beaver pats the mud with his paddle-tail;
Over the growing sugar . . . . over the cottonplant . . . . over the rice in
its low moist field;
Over the sharp-peaked farmhouse with its scalloped scum and slender
725   shoots from the gutters;
Over the western persimmon . . . . over the longleaved corn and the
delicate blue-flowered flax;
Over the white and brown buckwheat, a hummer and a buzzer there
with the rest,
Over the dusky green of the rye as it ripples and shades in the breeze;
Sealing mountains . . . . pulling myself cautiously up . . . . holding on by
low scragged limbs,
Walking the path worn in the grass and beat through the leaves of the
730   brush;
Where the quail is whistling betwixt the woods and the wheatlot,
Where the bat flies in the July eve . . . . where the great goldbug drops
through the dark;
Where the flails keep time on the barn floor,
Where the brook puts out of the roots of the old tree and flows to the
meadow,

Where cattle stand and shake away flies with the tremulous
    shuddering of their hides,   735
Where the cheese-cloth hangs in the kitchen, and andirons straddle
    the hearth-slab, and cobwebs fall in festoons from the rafters;
Where triphammers crash . . . . where the press is whirling its cylinders;
Wherever the human heart beats with terrible throes out of its ribs;
Where the pear-shaped balloon is floating aloft . . . . floating in it
    myself and looking composedly down;
Where the life-car is drawn on the slipnoose . . . . where the heat
    hatches pale-green eggs in the dented sand,   740
Where the she-whale swims with her calves and never forsakes them,
Where the steamship trails hindways its long pennant of smoke,
Where the ground-shark's fin cuts like a black chip out of the water,
Where the half-burned brig is riding on unknown currents,
Where shells grow to her slimy deck, and the dead are corrupting
    below;   745
Where the striped and starred flag is borne at the head of the
    regiments;
Approaching Manhattan, up by the long-stretching island,
Under Niagara, the cataract falling like a veil over my countenance;
Upon a door-step . . . . upon the horse-block of hard wood outside,
Upon the race-course, or enjoying pic-nics or jigs or a good game of
    base-ball,   750
At he-festivals with blackguard jibes and ironical license and bull-
    dances and drinking and laughter,
At the cider-mill, tasting the sweet of the brown sqush . . . . sucking the
    juice through a straw,
At apple-pealings, wanting kisses for all the red fruit I find,
At musters and beach-parties and friendly bees and huskings and
    house-raisings;
Where the mockingbird sounds his delicious gurgles, and cackles and
    screams and weeps,   755
Where the hay-rick stands in the barnyard, and the dry-stalks are
    scattered, and the brood cow waits in the hovel,
Where the bull advances to do his masculine work, and the stud to the
    mare, and the cock is treading the hen,

Where the heifers browse, and the geese nip their food with short
    jerks;
Where the sundown shadows lengthen over the limitless and lonesome
    prairie,
Where the herds of buffalo make a crawling spread of the square miles
760   far and near;
Where the hummingbird shimmers . . . . where the neck of the
    longlived swan is curving and winding;
Where the laughing-gull scoots by the slappy shore and laughs her
    near-human laugh;
Where beehives range on a gray bench in the garden half-hid by the
    high weeds;
Where the band-necked partridges roost in a ring on the ground with
    their heads out;
765 Where burial coaches enter the arched gates of a cemetery;
Where winter wolves bark amid wastes of snow and icicled trees;
Where the yellow-crowned heron comes to the edge of the marsh at
    night and feeds upon small crabs;
Where the splash of swimmers and divers cools the warm noon;
Where the katydid works her chromatic reed on the walnut-tree over
    the well;
770 Through patches of citrons and cucumbers with silver-wired leaves,
Through the salt-lick or orange glade . . . . or under conical firs;
Through the gymnasium . . . . through the curtained saloon . . . .
    through the office or public hall;
Pleased with the native and pleased with the foreign . . . . pleased with
    the new and old,
Pleased with women, the homely as well as the handsome,
Pleased with the quakeress as she puts off her bonnet and talks
775   melodiously,
Pleased with the primitive tunes of the choir of the whitewashed
    church,
Pleased with the earnest words of the sweating Methodist preacher, or
    any preacher . . . . looking seriously at the camp-meeting;
Looking in at the shop-windows in Broadway the whole forenoon . . . .
    pressing the flesh of my nose to the thick plate-glass,
Wandering the same afternoon with my face turned up to the clouds;

My right and left arms round the sides of two friends and I in the
    middle;   780
Coming home with the bearded and dark-cheeked bush-boy . . . .
    riding behind him at the drape of the day;
Far from the settlements studying the print of animals' feet, or the
    moccasin print;
By the cot in the hospital reaching lemonade to a feverish patient,
By the coffined corpse when all is still, examining with a candle;
Voyaging to every port to dicker and adventure;   785
Hurrying with the modern crowd, as eager and fickle as any,
Hot toward one I hate, ready in my madness to knife him;
Solitary at midnight in my back yard, my thoughts gone from me a
    long while,
Walking the old hills of Judea with the beautiful gentle god by my
    side;
Speeding through space . . . . speeding through heaven and the stars,   790
Speeding amid the seven satellites and the broad ring and the diameter
    of eighty thousand miles,
Speeding with tailed meteors . . . . throwing fire-balls like the rest,
Carrying the crescent child that carries its own full mother in its
    belly:
Storming enjoying planning loving cautioning,
Backing and filling, appearing and disappearing,   795
I tread day and night such roads.

I visit the orchards of God and look at the spheric product,
And look at quintillions ripened, and look at quintillions green.

I fly the flight of the fluid and swallowing soul,
My course runs below the soundings of plummets.   800

I help myself to material and immaterial,
No guard can shut me off, no law can prevent me.

I anchor my ship for a little while only,
My messengers continually cruise away or bring their returns to me.

I go hunting polar furs and the seal . . . . leaping chasms with a pike-
805   pointed staff . . . . clinging to topples of brittle and blue.

I ascend to the foretruck . . . . I take my place late at night in the crow's
    nest . . . . we sail through the arctic sea . . . . it is plenty light enough,
Through the clear atmosphere I stretch around on the wonderful
    beauty,
The enormous masses of ice pass me and I pass them . . . . the scenery
    is plain in all directions,
The white-topped mountains point up in the distance . . . . I fling out
    my fancies toward them;
We are about approaching some great battlefield in which we are soon
810   to be engaged,
We pass the colossal outposts of the encampments . . . . we pass with
    still feet and caution;
Or we are entering by the suburbs some vast and ruined city . . . . the
    blocks and fallen architecture more than all the living cities of the
    globe.

I am a free companion . . . . I bivouac by invading watchfires.

I turn the bridegroom out of bed and stay with the bride myself,
815 And tighten her all night to my thighs and lips.

My voice is the wife's voice, the screech by the rail of the stairs,
They fetch my man's body up dripping and drowned.

I understand the large hearts of heroes,
The courage of present times and all times;
How the skipper saw the crowded and rudderless wreck of the
820   steamship, and death chasing it up and down the storm,
How he knuckled tight and gave not back one inch, and was faithful of
    days and faithful of nights,
And chalked in large letters on a board, Be of good cheer, We will not
    desert you;
How he saved the drifting company at last,

How the lank loose-gowned women looked when boated from the side
    of their prepared graves,
How the silent old-faced infants, and the lifted sick, and the sharp-
    lipped unshaved men;   825
All this I swallow and it tastes good . . . . I like it well, and it becomes
    mine,
I am the man . . . . I suffered . . . . I was there.

The disdain and calmness of martyrs,
The mother condemned for a witch and burnt with dry wood, and her
    children gazing on;
The hounded slave that flags in the race and leans by the fence, blowing
    and covered with sweat,   830
The twinges that sting like needles his legs and neck,
The murderous buckshot and the bullets,
All these I feel or am.

I am the hounded slave . . . . I wince at the bite of the dogs,
Hell and despair are upon me . . . . crack and again crack the
    marksmen,   835
I clutch the rails of the fence . . . . my gore dribs thinned with the ooze
    of my skin,
I fall on the weeds and stones,
The riders spur their unwilling horses and haul close,
They taunt my dizzy ears . . . . they beat me violently over the head
    with their whip-stocks.

Agonies are one of my changes of garments;   840
I do not ask the wounded person how he feels . . . . I myself become the
    wounded person,
My hurt turns livid upon me as I lean on a cane and observe.

I am the mashed fireman with breastbone broken . . . . tumbling walls
    buried me in their debris,
Heat and smoke I inspired . . . . I heard the yelling shouts of my
    comrades,

845 I heard the distant click of their picks and shovels;
     They have cleared the beams away . . . . they tenderly lift me forth.

     I lie in the night air in my red shirt . . . . the pervading hush is for my
         sake,
     Painless after all I lie, exhausted but not so unhappy,
     White and beautiful are the faces around me . . . . the heads are bared
         of their fire-caps,
850 The kneeling crowd fades with the light of the torches.

     Distant and dead resuscitate,
     They show as the dial or move as the hands of me . . . . and I am the
         clock myself.

     I am an old artillerist, and tell of some fort's bombardment . . . . and
         am there again.

     Again the reveille of drummers . . . . again the attacking cannon and
         mortars and howitzers,
855 Again the attacked send their cannon responsive.

     I take part . . . . I see and hear the whole,
     The cries and curses and roar . . . . the plaudits for well aimed
         shots,
     The ambulanza slowly passing and trailing its red drip,
     Workmen searching after damages and to make indispensible
         repairs,
     The fall of grenades through the rent roof . . . . the fan-shaped
860   explosion,
     The whizz of limbs heads stone wood and iron high in the air.

     Again gurgles the mouth of my dying general . . . . he furiously waves
         with his hand,
     He gasps through the clot . . . . Mind not me . . . . mind . . . . the
         entrenchments.

I tell not the fall of Alamo . . . . not one escaped to tell the fall of
    Alamo,
The hundred and fifty are dumb yet at Alamo.   865

Hear now the tale of a jetblack sunrise,
Hear of the murder in cold blood of four hundred and twelve young men.

Retreating they had formed in a hollow square with their baggage for
    breastworks,
Nine hundred lives out of the surrounding enemy's nine times their
    number was the price they took in advance,
Their colonel was wounded and their ammunition gone,   870
They treated for an honorable capitulation, received writing and seal,
    gave up their arms, and marched back prisoners of war.

They were the glory of the race of rangers,
Matchless with a horse, a rifle, a song, a supper or a courtship,
Large, turbulent, brave, handsome, generous, proud and affectionate,
Bearded, sunburnt, dressed in the free costume of hunters,   875
Not a single one over thirty years of age.

The second Sunday morning they were brought out in squads and
    massacred . . . . it was beautiful early summer,
The work commenced about five o'clock and was over by eight.

None obeyed the command to kneel,
Some made a mad and helpless rush . . . . some stood stark and
    straight,   880
A few fell at once, shot in the temple or heart . . . . the living and dead
    lay together,
The maimed and mangled dug in the dirt . . . . the new-comers saw
    them there;
Some half-killed attempted to crawl away,
These were dispatched with bayonets or battered with the blunts of
    muskets;

A youth not seventeen years old seized his assassin till two more came
885   to release him,
The three were all torn, and covered with the boy's blood.

At eleven o'clock began the burning of the bodies;
And that is the tale of the murder of the four hundred and twelve
    young men,
And that was a jetblack sunrise.

890 Did you read in the seabooks of the oldfashioned frigate-fight?
Did you learn who won by the light of the moon and stars?

Our foe was no skulk in his ship, I tell you,
His was the English pluck, and there is no tougher or truer, and never
    was, and never will be;
Along the lowered eve he came, horribly raking us.

We closed with him . . . . the yards entangled . . . . the cannon
895   touched,
My captain lashed fast with his own hands.

We had received some eighteen-pound shots under the water,
On our lower-gun-deck two large pieces had burst at the first fire,
    killing all around and blowing up overhead.

Ten o'clock at night, and the full moon shining and the leaks on the
    gain, and five feet of water reported,
The master-at-arms loosing the prisoners confined in the after-hold to
900   give them a chance for themselves.

The transit to and from the magazine was now stopped by the
    sentinels,
They saw so many strange faces they did not know whom to
    trust.

Our frigate was afire . . . . the other asked if we demanded quarters? if
    our colors were struck and the fighting done?

I laughed content when I heard the voice of my little captain,
We have not struck, he composedly cried, We have just begun our part
    of the fighting.   905

Only three guns were in use,
One was directed by the captain himself against the enemy's
    mainmast,
Two well-served with grape and canister silenced his musketry and
    cleared his decks,

The tops alone seconded the fire of this little battery, especially the
    maintop,
They all held out bravely during the whole of the action.   910

Not a moment's cease,
The leaks gained fast on the pumps . . . . the fire eat toward the
    powder-magazine,
One of the pumps was shot away . . . . it was generally thought we were
    sinking.

Serene stood the little captain,
He was not hurried . . . . his voice was neither high nor low,   915
His eyes gave more light to us than our battle-lanterns.

Toward twelve at night, there in the beams of the moon they
    surrendered to us.

Stretched and still lay the midnight,
Two great hulls motionless on the breast of the darkness,
Our vessel riddled and slowly sinking . . . . preparations to pass to the
    one we had conquered,   920

The captain on the quarter deck coldly giving his orders through a
    countenance white as a sheet,
Near by the corpse of the child that served in the cabin,
The dead face of an old salt with long white hair and carefully curled
    whiskers,
The flames spite of all that could be done flickering aloft and below,
925 The husky voices of the two or three officers yet fit for duty,
Formless stacks of bodies and bodies by themselves . . . . dabs of flesh
    upon the masts and spars,
The cut of cordage and dangle of rigging . . . . the slight shock of the
    soothe of waves,
Black and impassive guns, and litter of powder-parcels, and the strong
    scent,
Delicate sniffs of the seabreeze . . . . smells of sedgy grass and fields by
    the shore . . . . death-messages given in charge to survivors,
930 The hiss of the surgeon's knife and the gnawing teeth of his saw,
The wheeze, the cluck, the swash of falling blood . . . . the short wild
    scream, the long dull tapering groan,
These so . . . . these irretrievable.

O Christ! My fit is mastering me!
What the rebel said gaily adjusting his throat to the rope-noose,
What the savage at the stump, his eye-sockets empty, his mouth
935   spirting whoops and defiance,
What stills the traveler come to the vault at Mount Vernon,
What sobers the Brooklyn boy as he looks down the shores of the
    Wallabout and remembers the prison ships,
What burnt the gums of the redcoat at Saratoga when he surrendered
    his brigades,
These become mine and me every one, and they are but little,
940 I become as much more as I like.

I become any presence or truth of humanity here,
And see myself in prison shaped like another man,
And feel the dull unintermitted pain.

For me the keepers of convicts shoulder their carbines and keep
    watch,
It is I let out in the morning and barred at night.   945

Not a mutineer walks handcuffed to the jail, but I am handcuffed to
    him and walk by his side,
I am less the jolly one there, and more the silent one with sweat on my
    twitching lips.

Not a youngster is taken for larceny, but I go up too and am tried and
    sentenced.

Not a cholera patient lies at the last gasp, but I also lie at the last
    gasp,
My face is ash-colored, my sinews gnarl . . . . away from me people
    retreat.   950

Askers embody themselves in me, and I am embodied in them,
I project my hat and sit shamefaced and beg.

I rise extatic through all, and sweep with the true gravitation,
The whirling and whirling is elemental within me.

Somehow I have been stunned. Stand back!   955
Give me a little time beyond my cuffed head and slumbers and dreams
    and gaping,
I discover myself on a verge of the usual mistake.

That I could forget the mockers and insults!
That I could forget the trickling tears and the blows of the bludgeons
    and hammers!
That I could look with a separate look on my own crucifixion and
    bloody crowning!   960

I remember . . . . I resume the overstaid fraction,
The grave of rock multiplies what has been confided to it . . . . or to any
  graves,
The corpses rise . . . . the gashes heal . . . . the fastenings roll away.

I troop forth replenished with supreme power, one of an average
  unending procession,
We walk the roads of Ohio and Massachusetts and Virginia and
  Wisconsin and New York and New Orleans and Texas and Montreal
965   and San Francisco and Charleston and Savannah and Mexico,
Inland and by the seacoast and boundary lines . . . . and we pass the
  boundary lines.

Our swift ordinances are on their way over the whole earth,
The blossoms we wear in our hats are the growth of two thousand years.

Eleves I salute you,
I see the approach of your numberless gangs . . . . I see you understand
970   yourselves and me,
And know that they who have eyes are divine, and the blind and lame
  are equally divine,
And that my steps drag behind yours yet go before them,
And are aware how I am with you no more than I am with everybody.

The friendly and flowing savage . . . . Who is he?
975 Is he waiting for civilization or past it and mastering it?

Is he some southwesterner raised outdoors? Is he Canadian?
Is he from the Mississippi country? or from Iowa, Oregon or
  California? or from the mountains? or prairie life or bush-life? or
  from the sea?

Wherever he goes men and women accept and desire him,
They desire he should like them and touch them and speak to them
  and stay with them.

Behaviour lawless as snow-flakes . . . . words simple as grass . . . .
    uncombed head and laughter and naivete;   980
Slowstepping feet and the common features, and the common modes
    and emanations,
They descend in new forms from the tips of his fingers,
They are wafted with the odor of his body or breath . . . . they fly out of
    the glance of his eyes.

Flaunt of the sunshine I need not your bask . . . . lie over,
You light surfaces only . . . . I force the surfaces and the depths also.   985

Earth! you seem to look for something at my hands,
Say old topknot! what do you want?

Man or woman! I might tell how I like you, but cannot,
And might tell what it is in me and what it is in you, but cannot,
And might tell the pinings I have . . . . the pulse of my nights and days.   990

Behold I do not give lectures or a little charity,
What I give I give out of myself.

You there, impotent, loose in the knees, open your scarfed chops till I
    blow grit within you,
Spread your palms and lift the flaps of your pockets,
I am not to be denied . . . . I compel . . . . I have stores plenty and to
    spare,   995
And any thing I have I bestow.

I do not ask who you are . . . . that is not important to me,
You can do nothing and be nothing but what I will infold you.

To a drudge of the cottonfields or emptier of privies I lean . . . . on his
    right cheek I put the family kiss,
And in my soul I swear I never will deny him.   1000

On women fit for conception I start bigger and nimbler babes,
This day I am jetting the stuff of far more arrogant republics.

To any one dying . . . . thither I speed and twist the knob of the
    door,
Turn the bedclothes toward the foot of the bed,
1005 Let the physician and the priest go home.

I seize the descending man . . . . I raise him with resistless will.

O despairer, here is my neck,
By God! you shall not go down! Hang your whole weight upon me.

I dilate you with tremendous breath . . . . I buoy you up;
Every room of the house do I fill with an armed force . . . . lovers of me,
1010   bafflers of graves:
Sleep! I and they keep guard all night;
Not doubt, not decease shall dare to lay finger upon you,
I have embraced you, and henceforth possess you to myself,
And when you rise in the morning you will find what I tell you is so.

1015 I am he bringing help for the sick as they pant on their backs,
And for strong upright men I bring yet more needed help.

I heard what was said of the universe,
Heard it and heard of several thousand years;
It is middling well as far as it goes . . . . but is that all?

1020 Magnifying and applying come I,
Outbidding at the start the old cautious hucksters,
The most they offer for mankind and eternity less than a spirt of my
    own seminal wet,
Taking myself the exact dimensions of Jehovah and laying them
    away,

Lithographing Kronos and Zeus his son, and Hercules his
    grandson,
Buying drafts of Osiris and Isis and Belus and Brahma and Adonai,   1025
In my portfolio placing Manito loose, and Allah on a leaf, and the
    crucifix engraved,
With Odin, and the hideous-faced Mexitli, and all idols and
    images,
Honestly taking them all for what they are worth, and not a cent
    more,
Admitting they were alive and did the work of their day,
Admitting they bore mites as for unfledged birds who have now to rise
    and fly and sing for themselves,   1030
Accepting the rough deific sketches to fill out better in myself . . . .
    bestowing them freely on each man and woman I see,
Discovering as much or more in a framer framing a house,
Putting higher claims for him there with his rolled-up sleeves, driving
    the mallet and chisel;
Not objecting to special revelations . . . . considering a curl of smoke or
    a hair on the back of my hand as curious as any revelation;
Those ahold of fire-engines and hook-and-ladder ropes more to me
    than the gods of the antique wars,   1035
Minding their voices peal through the crash of destruction,
Their brawny limbs passing safe over charred laths . . . . their white
    foreheads whole and unhurt out of the flames;
By the mechanic's wife with her babe at her nipple interceding for
    every person born;
Three scythes at harvest whizzing in a row from three lusty angels with
    shirts bagged out at their waists;
The snag-toothed hostler with red hair redeeming sins past and to
    come,   1040
Selling all he possesses and traveling on foot to fee lawyers for his
    brother and sit by him while he is tried for forgery:
What was strewn in the amplest strewing the square rod about me,
    and not filling the square rod then;
The bull and the bug never worshipped half enough,
Dung and dirt more admirable than was dreamed,

The supernatural of no account . . . . myself waiting my time to be one
1045   of the supremes,
The day getting ready for me when I shall do as much good as the best,
and be as prodigious,
Guessing when I am it will not tickle me much to receive puffs out of
pulpit or print;
By my life-lumps! becoming already a creator!
Putting myself here and now to the ambushed womb of the shadows!

1050   . . . . A call in the midst of the crowd,
My own voice, orotund sweeping and final.

Come my children,
Come my boys and girls, and my women and household and intimates,
Now the performer launches his nerve . . . . he has passed his prelude
on the reeds within.

Easily written loosefingered chords! I feel the thrum of their climax
1055   and close.

My head evolves on my neck,
Music rolls, but not from the organ . . . . folks are around me, but they
are no household of mine.

Ever the hard and unsunk ground,
Ever the eaters and drinkers . . . . ever the upward and downward
sun . . . . ever the air and the ceaseless tides,
1060   Ever myself and my neighbors, refreshing and wicked and real,
Ever the old inexplicable query . . . . ever that thorned thumb—that
breath of itches and thirsts,
Ever the vexer's hoot! hoot! till we find where the sly one hides and
bring him forth;
Ever love . . . . ever the sobbing liquid of life,
Ever the bandage under the chin . . . . ever the tressels of death.

Here and there with dimes on the eyes walking,   1065
To feed the greed of the belly the brains liberally spooning,
Tickets buying or taking or selling, but in to the feast never once
    going;
Many sweating and ploughing and thrashing, and then the chaff for
    payment receiving,
A few idly owning, and they the wheat continually claiming.

This is the city . . . . and I am one of the citizens;   1070
Whatever interests the rest interests me . . . . politics, churches,
    newspapers, schools,
Benevolent societies, improvements, banks, tariffs, steamships,
    factories, markets,
Stocks and stores and real estate and personal estate.

They who piddle and patter here in collars and tailed coats . . . . I am
    aware who they are . . . . and that they are not worms or fleas,
I acknowledge the duplicates of myself under all the scrape-lipped and
    pipe-legged concealments.   1075

The weakest and shallowest is deathless with me,
What I do and say the same waits for them,
Every thought that flounders in me the same flounders in them.

I know perfectly well my own egotism,
And know my omniverous words, and cannot say any less,   1080
And would fetch you whoever you are flush with myself.

My words are words of a questioning, and to indicate reality;
This printed and bound book . . . . but the printer and the printing-
    office boy?
The marriage estate and settlement . . . . but the body and mind of the
    bridegroom? also those of the bride?
The panorama of the sea . . . . but the sea itself?   1085

The well-taken photographs . . . . but your wife or friend close and solid
    in your arms?
The fleet of ships of the line and all the modern improvements . . . . but
    the craft and pluck of the admiral?
The dishes and fare and furniture . . . . but the host and hostess, and
    the look out of their eyes?
The sky up there . . . . yet here or next door or across the way?
1090 The saints and sages in history . . . . but you yourself?
Sermons and creeds and theology . . . . but the human brain, and what
    is called reason, and what is called love, and what is called life?

I do not despise you priests;
My faith is the greatest of faiths and the least of faiths,
Enclosing all worship ancient and modern, and all between ancient
    and modern,
1095 Believing I shall come again upon the earth after five thousand years,
Waiting responses from oracles . . . . honoring the gods . . . . saluting
    the sun,
Making a fetish of the first rock or stump . . . . powowing with sticks in
    the circle of obis,
Helping the lama or brahmin as he trims the lamps of the idols,
Dancing yet through the streets in a phallic procession . . . . rapt and
    austere in the woods, a gymnosophist,
Drinking mead from the skull-cup . . . . to shasta and vedas
1100   admirant . . . . minding the koran,
Walking the teokallis, spotted with gore from the stone and knife—
    beating the serpent-skin drum;
Accepting the gospels, accepting him that was crucified, knowing
    assuredly that he is divine,
To the mass kneeling—to the puritan's prayer rising—sitting patiently
    in a pew,
Ranting and frothing in my insane crisis—waiting dead-like till my
    spirit arouses me;
Looking forth on pavement and land, and outside of pavement and
1105   land,
Belonging to the winders of the circuit of circuits.

One of that centripetal and centrifugal gang,
I turn and talk like a man leaving charges before a journey.

Down-hearted doubters, dull and excluded,
Frivolous sullen moping angry affected disheartened atheistical,   1110
I know every one of you, and know the unspoken interrogatories,
By experience I know them.

How the flukes splash!
How they contort rapid as lightning, with spasms and spouts of
    blood!

Be at peace bloody flukes of doubters and sullen mopers,   1115
I take my place among you as much as among any;

The past is the push of you and me and all precisely the same,
And the night is for you and me and all,
And what is yet untried and afterward is for you and me and all.

I do not know what is untried and afterward,   1120
But I know it is sure and alive and sufficient.

Each who passes is considered, and each who stops is considered, and
    not a single one can it fail.

It cannot fail the young man who died and was buried,
Nor the young woman who died and was put by his side,
Nor the little child that peeped in at the door and then drew back and
    was never seen again,   1125
Nor the old man who has lived without purpose, and feels it with
    bitterness worse than gall,
Nor him in the poorhouse tubercled by rum and the bad disorder,
Nor the numberless slaughtered and wrecked . . . . nor the brutish
    koboo, called the ordure of humanity,

Nor the sacs merely floating with open mouths for food to slip in,
Nor any thing in the earth, or down in the oldest graves of the
1130   earth,
Nor any thing in the myriads of spheres, nor one of the myriads of
    myriads that in-habit them,
Nor the present, nor the least wisp that is known.

It is time to explain myself . . . . let us stand up.

What is known I strip away . . . . I launch all men and women forward
    with me into the unknown.

1135 The clock indicates the moment . . . . but what does eternity indicate?

Eternity lies in bottomless reservoirs . . . . its buckets are rising forever
    and ever,
They pour and they pour and they exhale away.

We have thus far exhausted trillions of winters and summers;
There are trillions ahead, and trillions ahead of them.

1140 Births have brought us richness and variety,
And other births will bring us richness and variety.

I do not call one greater and one smaller,
That which fills its period and place is equal to any.

Were mankind murderous or jealous upon you my brother or my
    sister?

1145 I am sorry for you . . . . they are not murderous or jealous upon me;
All has been gentle with me . . . . I keep no account with lamentation;
What have I to do with lamentation?

I am an acme of things accomplished, and I an encloser of things
    to be.

My feet strike an apex of the apices of the stairs,
On every step bunches of ages, and larger bunches between the
    steps,   1150
All below duly traveled—and still I mount and mount.

Rise after rise bow the phantoms behind me,
Afar down I see the huge first Nothing, the vapor from the nostrils of
    death,
I know I was even there . . . . I waited unseen and always,
And slept while God carried me through the lethargic mist,   1155
And took my time . . . . and took no hurt from the foetid carbon.

Long I was hugged close . . . . long and long.

Immense have been the preparations for me,
Faithful and friendly the arms that have helped me.

Cycles ferried my cradle, rowing and rowing like cheerful
    boatmen;   1160
For room to me stars kept aside in their own rings,
They sent influences to look after what was to hold me.

Before I was born out of my mother generations guided me,
My embryo has never been torpid . . . . nothing could overlay it;
For it the nebula cohered to an orb . . . . the long slow strata piled to
    rest it on . . . . vast vegetables gave it sustenance,   1165
Monstrous sauroids transported it in their mouths and deposited it
    with care.

All forces have been steadily employed to complete and delight me,
Now I stand on this spot with my soul.

Span of youth! Ever-pushed elasticity! Manhood balanced and florid
    and full!

1170 My lovers suffocate me!
    Crowding my lips, and thick in the pores of my skin,
    Jostling me through streets and public halls . . . . coming naked to me
      at night,
    Crying by day Ahoy from the rocks of the river . . . . swinging and
      chirping over my head,
    Calling my name from flowerbeds or vines or tangled underbrush,
    Or while I swim in the bath . . . . or drink from the pump at the
      corner . . . . or the curtain is down at the opera . . . . or I glimpse at a
1175   woman's face in the railroad car;
    Lighting on every moment of my life,
    Bussing my body with soft and balsamic busses,
    Noiselessly passing handfuls out of their hearts and giving them to be
      mine.

Old age superbly rising! Ineffable grace of dying days!

Every condition promulges not only itself . . . . it promulges what grows
1180   after and out of itself,
    And the dark hush promulges as much as any.

I open my scuttle at night and see the far-sprinkled systems,
    And all I see, multiplied as high as I can cipher, edge but the rim of the
      farther systems.

Wider and wider they spread, expanding and always expanding,
1185 Outward and outward and forever outward.

My sun has his sun, and round him obediently wheels,
    He joins with his partners a group of superior circuit,
    And greater sets follow, making specks of the greatest inside them.

There is no stoppage, and never can be stoppage;
If I and you and the worlds and all beneath or upon their surfaces, and
    all the palpable life, were this moment reduced back to a pallid float,
    it would not avail in the long run, 1190
We should surely bring up again where we now stand,
And as surely go as much farther, and then farther and farther.

A few quadrillions of eras, a few octillions of cubic leagues, do not
    hazard the span, or make it impatient,
They are but parts . . . . any thing is but a part.

See ever so far . . . . there is limitless space outside of that, 1195
Count ever so much . . . . there is limitless time around that.

Our rendezvous is fitly appointed . . . . God will be there and wait till
    we come.

I know I have the best of time and space—and that I was never
    measured, and never will be measured.

I tramp a perpetual journey,
My signs are a rain-proof coat and good shoes and a staff cut from the
    woods; 1200
No friend of mine takes his ease in my chair,
I have no chair, nor church nor philosophy;
I lead no man to a dinner-table or library or exchange,

But each man and each woman of you I lead upon a knoll,
My left hand hooks you round the waist, 1205
My right hand points to landscapes of continents, and a plain public
    road.

Not I, not any one else can travel that road for you,
You must travel it for yourself.

It is not far . . . . it is within reach,
1210 Perhaps you have been on it since you were born, and did not know,
Perhaps it is every where on water and on land.

Shoulder your duds, and I will mine, and let us hasten forth;
Wonderful cities and free nations we shall fetch as we go.

If you tire, give me both burdens, and rest the chuff of your hand on
     my hip,
1215 And in due time you shall repay the same service to me;
For after we start we never lie by again.

This day before dawn I ascended a hill and looked at the crowded
     heaven,
And I said to my spirit, When we become the enfolders of those orbs
     and the pleasure and knowledge of every thing in them, shall we be
     filled and satisfied then?
And my spirit said No, we level that lift to pass and continue beyond.

1220 You are also asking me questions, and I hear you;
I answer that I cannot answer . . . . you must find out for yourself.

Sit awhile wayfarer,
Here are biscuits to eat and here is milk to drink,
But as soon as you sleep and renew yourself in sweet clothes I will
     certainly kiss you with my goodbye kiss and open the gate for your
     egress hence.

1225 Long enough have you dreamed contemptible dreams,
Now I wash the gum from your eyes,
You must habit yourself to the dazzle of the light and of every moment
     of your life.

Long have you timidly waded, holding a plank by the shore,
Now I will you to be a bold swimmer,

To jump off in the midst of the sea, and rise again and nod to me and
    shout, and laughingly dash with your hair.   1230

I am the teacher of athletes,
He that by me spreads a wider breast than my own proves the width of
    my own,
He most honors my style who learns under it to destroy the teacher.

The boy I love, the same becomes a man not through derived power
    but in his own right,
Wicked, rather than virtuous out of conformity or fear,   1235
Fond of his sweetheart, relishing well his steak,
Unrequited love or a slight cutting him worse than a wound cuts,
First rate to ride, to fight, to hit the bull's eye, to sail a skiff, to sing a
    song or play on the banjo,
Preferring scars and faces pitted with smallpox over all latherers and
    those that keep out of the sun.

I teach straying from me, yet who can stray from me?   1240
I follow you whoever you are from the present hour;
My words itch at your ears till you understand them.

I do not say these things for a dollar, or to fill up the time while I wait
    for a boat;
It is you talking just as much as myself . . . . I act as the tongue of you,
It was tied in your mouth . . . . in mine it begins to be loosened.   1245

I swear I will never mention love or death inside a house,
And I swear I never will translate myself at all, only to him or her who
    privately stays with me in the open air.

If you would understand me go to the heights or water-shore,
The nearest gnat is an explanation and a drop or the motion of waves
    a key,
The maul the oar and the handsaw second my words.   1250

No shuttered room or school can commune with me,
But roughs and little children better than they.

The young mechanic is closest to me . . . . he knows me pretty well,
The woodman that takes his axe and jug with him shall take me with
    him all day,
1255 The farmboy ploughing in the field feels good at the sound of my voice,
In vessels that sail my words must sail . . . . I go with fishermen and
    seamen, and love them,
My face rubs to the hunter's face when he lies down alone in his
    blanket,
The driver thinking of me does not mind the jolt of his wagon,
The young mother and old mother shall comprehend me,
The girl and the wife rest the needle a moment and forget where
1260   they are,
They and all would resume what I have told them.

I have said that the soul is not more than the body,
And I have said that the body is not more than the soul,
And nothing, not God, is greater to one than one's-self is,
And whoever walks a furlong without sympathy walks to his own
1265   funeral, dressed in his shroud,
And I or you pocketless of a dime may purchase the pick of the earth,
And to glance with an eye or show a bean in its pod confounds the
    learning of all times,
And there is no trade or employment but the young man following it
    may become a hero,
And there is no object so soft but it makes a hub for the wheeled
    universe,
And any man or woman shall stand cool and supercilious before a
1270   million universes.

And I call to mankind, Be not curious about God,
For I who am curious about each am not curious about God,
No array of terms can say how much I am at peace about God and
    about death.

I hear and behold God in every object, yet I understand God not in the
    least,
Nor do I understand who there can be more wonderful than myself.   1275

Why should I wish to see God better than this day?
I see something of God each hour of the twenty-four, and each
    moment then,
In the faces of men and women I see God, and in my own face in the
    glass;
I find letters from God dropped in the street, and every one is signed
    by God's name,
And I leave them where they are, for I know that others will punctually
    come forever and ever.   1280

And as to you death, and you bitter hug of mortality . . . . it is idle to try
    to alarm me.

To his work without flinching the accoucheur comes,
I see the elderhand pressing receiving supporting,
I recline by the sills of the exquisite flexible doors . . . . and mark the
    outlet, and mark the relief and escape.

And as to you corpse I think you are good manure, but that does not
    offend me,   1285
I smell the white roses sweetscented and growing,
I reach to the leafy lips . . . . I reach to the polished breasts of
    melons.

And as to you life, I reckon you are the leavings of many deaths,
No doubt I have died myself ten thousand times before.

I hear you whispering there O stars of heaven,   1290
O suns . . . . O grass of graves . . . . O perpetual transfers and
    promotions . . . . if you do not say anything how can I say
    anything?

Of the turbid pool that lies in the autumn forest,
Of the moon that descends the steeps of the soughing twilight,
Toss, sparkles of day and dusk .... toss on the black stems that decay
in the muck,
1295 Toss to the moaning gibberish of the dry limbs.

I ascend from the moon .... I ascend from the night,
And perceive of the ghastly glitter the sunbeams reflected,
And debouch to the steady and central from the offspring great or
small.

There is that in me .... I do not know what it is .... but I know it is
in me.

1300 Wrenched and sweaty .... calm and cool then my body becomes;
I sleep .... I sleep long.

I do not know it .... it is without name .... it is a word unsaid,
It is not in any dictionary or utterance or symbol.

Something it swings on more than the earth I swing on,
1305 To it the creation is the friend whose embracing awakes me.

Perhaps I might tell more .... Outlines! I plead for my brothers and
sisters.

Do you see O my brothers and sisters?
It is not chaos or death .... it is form and union and plan .... it is
eternal life .... it is happiness.

The past and present wilt .... I have filled them and emptied
them,
1310 And proceed to fill my next fold of the future.

Listener up there! Here you . . . . what have you to confide to me?
Look in my face while I snuff the sidle of evening,
Talk honestly, for no one else hears you, and I stay only a minute
    longer.

Do I contradict myself?
Very well then . . . . I contradict myself;   1315
I am large . . . . I contain multitudes.

I concentrate toward them that are nigh . . . . I wait on the door-slab.

Who has done his day's work and will soonest be through with his
    supper?
Who wishes to walk with me?

Will you speak before I am gone? Will you prove already too late?   1320

The spotted hawk swoops by and accuses me . . . . he complains of my
    gab and my loitering.

I too am not a bit tamed . . . . I too am untranslatable,
I sound my barbaric yawp over the roofs of the world.

The last scud of day holds back for me,
It flings my likeness after the rest and true as any on the shadowed
    wilds,   1325
It coaxes me to the vapor and the dusk.

I depart as air . . . . I shake my white locks at the runaway sun,
I effuse my flesh in eddies and drift it in lacy jags.

I bequeath myself to the dirt to grow from the grass I love,
If you want me again look for me under your bootsoles.   1330

You will hardly know who I am or what I mean,
But I shall be good health to you nevertheless,
And filter and fibre your blood.

Failing to fetch me at first keep encouraged,
1335 Missing me one place search another,
I stop some where waiting for you

Bibliography

Acknowledgments

Index

Bibliography

Allen, Gay Wilson. *The Solitary Singer: A Critical Biography of Walt Whitman.* New York: New York University Press, 1955.

Anderson, Quentin. *The Imperial Self: An Essay in American Literary and Cultural History.* New York: Knopf, 1971.

Bauerlein, Mark. *Whitman and the American Idiom.* Baton Rouge: Louisiana State University Press, 1991.

Black, Stephen. *Whitman's Journey into Chaos.* Princeton, NJ: Princeton University Press, 1975.

Bloom, Harold. *Agon: Towards a Theory of Revisionism.* New York: Oxford University Press, 1982.

———. *Possessed by Memory: The Inward Light of Criticism.* New York: Knopf, 2019.

Cantor, Paul. *Pop Culture and the Dark Side of the American Dream: Con Men, Gangsters, Drug Lords, and Zombies.* Lexington: University Press of Kentucky, 2019.

Chase, Richard. *Walt Whitman Reconsidered.* New York: William Sloane, 1955.

Christy, Arthur. *The Orient in American Transcendentalism: A Study of Emerson, Thoreau, and Alcott.* New York: Columbia University Press, 1932.

Cowley, Malcolm. Introduction to *Walt Whitman's Leaves of Grass: The First (1855) Edition,* vii–xxxvii. New York: Viking, 1959.

Emerson, Ralph Waldo. *Essays and Lectures.* New York: Library of America, 1983.

Epstein, Daniel Mark. *Lincoln and Whitman: Parallel Lives in Civil War Washington.* New York: Random House, 2005.

Erkkila, Betsy. *Whitman the Political Poet.* New York: Oxford University Press, 1989.

Feidelson, Charles. *Symbolism and American Literature.* Chicago: University of Chicago Press, 1953.

Fletcher, Angus. "The Book of a Lifetime." In *A New Literary History of America,* edited by Greil Marcus and Werner Sollors, 306–312. Cambridge, MA: Harvard University Press, 2009.

———. *A New Theory for American Poetry: Democracy, the Environment and the Future of Imagination.* Cambridge, MA: Harvard University Press, 2004.

Folsom, Ed. *Walt Whitman's Native Representations.* Cambridge: Cambridge University Press, 1994.

Freud, Sigmund. *Standard Edition of the Complete Psychological Works.* Edited and translated by James Strachey et al. 24 vols. London: Hogarth, 1953–1974.

Genoways, Ted. *Walt Whitman and the Civil War: America's Poet during the Lost Years of 1860–1862.* Berkeley: University of California Press, 2009.

Irwin, John. *American Hieroglyphics: The Symbol of the Egyptian Hieroglyphic in the American Renaissance.* New Haven, CT: Yale University Press, 1980.

James, William. *The Varieties of Religious Experience.* New York: Collier Books, 1961.

Kaplan, Harold. *Democratic Humanism and American Literature.* Chicago: University of Chicago Press, 1972.

Kaplan, Justin. *Walt Whitman: A Life.* New York: Simon and Schuster, 1980.

Larson, Kerry C. *Whitman's Drama of Consciousness.* Chicago: University of Chicago Press, 1988.

Lewis, R. W. B. *The American Adam: Innocence, Tragedy, and Tradition in the Nineteenth Century.* Chicago: University of Chicago Press, 1955.

Loving, Jerome M. *Emerson, Whitman, and the American Muse.* Chapel Hill: University of North Carolina Press, 1982.

Martin, Justin. *Rebel Souls: Walt Whitman and America's First Bohemians.* Boston: De Capo, 2014.

Matthiessen, F. O. *American Renaissance.* New York: Oxford University Press, 1941.

Miller, James E., Jr. "*Song of Myself* as Inverted Mystical Experience." *PMLA* 70 (September 1955): 636–661.

Moon, Michael. *Disseminating Whitman: Revision and Corporeality in "Leaves of Grass."* Cambridge, MA: Harvard University Press, 1991.

Morris, Roy, Jr. *The Better Angel: Walt Whitman in the Civil War.* New York: Oxford University Press, 2000.

O'Connor, William. *The Good Gray Poet.* New York: Bunce and Huntington, 1866.

Paglia, Camille. *Break, Blow, Burn.* New York: Random House, 2005.

Poirier, Richard. *Trying It Out in America: Literary and Other Performances.* New York: Farrar, Straus and Giroux, 1999.

Reynolds, David S. *Walt Whitman's America: A Cultural Biography.* New York: Knopf, 1995.

Rivera, Diego. *My Art, My Life: An Autobiography.* New York: Dover, 1991.

Rorty, Richard. *Achieving Our Country: Leftist Thought in Twentieth-Century America.* Cambridge, MA: Harvard University Press, 1998.

Shively, Charley. *Calamus Lovers: Walt Whitman's Working Class Camerados.* San Francisco: Gay Sunshine, 1987.

Stevens, Wallace. *The Palm at the End of the Mind: Selected Poems and a Play.* Edited by Holly Stevens. New York: Vintage Books, 1971.

Stovall, Floyd. *The Foreground of Leaves of Grass.* Charlottesville: University of Virginia Press, 1974.

Thomas, M. Wynn. *The Lunar Light of Whitman's Poetry.* Cambridge, MA: Harvard University Press, 1987.

Thoreau, Henry David. *Walden.* New York: Random House, 2016.

Traubel, Horace. *With Walt Whitman in Camden.* 9 vols. New York: Rowman and Littlefield, 1906–1996.

Twain, Mark. *The Autobiography of Mark Twain.* 3 vols. Berkeley: University of California Press, 2013.

Wardrop, Daneen. *Word, Birth and Culture: The Poetry of Poe, Whitman, and Dickinson.* Westport, CT: Greenwood, 2002.

Warren, James Perrin. *Walt Whitman's Language Experiment.* University Park: Pennsylvania State University Press, 1990

Whitman, Walt. *Complete Poetry and Collected Prose.* New York: Library of America, 1982.

———. *The Correspondence, 1842–1867.* Edited by Edwin Haviland Miller. New York: New York University Press, 1961.

———. *Notebooks and Unpublished Prose Manuscripts.* Edited by Edward F. Grier. New York: New York University Press, 1984.

———. *Song of Myself: And Other Poems by Walt Whitman.* Selected and introduced by Robert Hass. With a lexicon of the poem by Robert Hass and Paul Ebenkamp. Berkeley: Counterpoint, 2010.

———. *Song of Myself: With a Complete Commentary.* Introduction and commentary by Ed Folsom and Christopher Merrill. Iowa City: University of Iowa Press, 2016.

———. *The Walt Whitman Archive.* Edited by Matt Cohen, Ed Folsom, and Kenneth M. Price. http://www.whitmanarchive.org/.

Wilson, Ivy G., ed. *Whitman Noir: Black America and the Good Gray Poet.* Iowa City: University of Iowa Press, 2014.

Zweig, Paul. *Walt Whitman: The Making of the Poet.* New York: Basic Books, 1985.

Acknowledgments

Thanks first to my editor, Lindsay Waters, for his loyalty, energy, and intelligence. And for invaluable assistance in moving the book forward, thanks to Lindsay's associates Louise Robbins and Joy Deng.

I'm grateful to my colleague Steve Cushman, who generously read an early version of the manuscript and made numerous extremely intelligent and helpful suggestions. David Mikics read the book when it was close to completion and offered consequential advice. Thanks too to the three readers for Harvard University Press, who offered valuable responses.

Some of the ideas explored in this book were initially considered in "Walt Whitman's Guide to a Thriving Democracy," *Atlantic,* May 2019, pp. 100–110.

The existence of the book is in part due to my students at the University of Virginia, who worked through *Song of Myself* with me, page by page, line by line. Thank you.

Thanks to Matthew Martello, who provided expert research help and splendid conversation to boot. Thank you to Nora Pehrson, who contributed a great deal to preparing the manuscript.

I'm grateful to Josh Hall, who invited me to San Diego University to give three lectures on Whitman in the Illume-Knapp series. He provided memorable hospitality and wonderful talk. He and his wife, Dianna, were splendid hosts.

Thanks to Whitman scholar Ed Folsom for generously answering my questions about the poet.

I'm grateful to Michael Pollan for conversation on the subject of Whitman and many other matters. We have been friends for fifty years.

Thanks to my family, now blissfully larger than it was the last time I wrote an acknowledgments page—Matthew and Anna, William and Ashley—and my wife, Liz, who has given me so much.

I have the good fortune to teach at the University of Virginia, where my appointment as University Professor has given me time and resources to do my work under conditions that are close to ideal. Thanks to John Casteen III, former president of the University of Virginia, for granting the appointment, and thanks to James Ryan, our current president, for overseeing it now.

Thanks, down the long roads of time, to the University of Virginia's founder, Thomas Jefferson, who wrote, "This institution will be based on the illimitable freedom of the human mind, for here we are not afraid to follow truth wherever it may lead, nor to tolerate any error so long as reason is left free to combat it."

Index

abasement, as chief sin in Whitman's
    view, 74–75
Aeneid (Virgil), 17
Alamo, fall of, 72–73
animals, Whitman's affection for and
    use of to satirize human character-
    istics, 66–68
aristocracy: Twain's view of, 59;
    Whitman's view of, xii, 5–6, 19,
    25, 37, 42, 59, 67, 100. *See also*
    feudalism
Armory Square Hospital, 121, 122, 131
atheism, Whitman and, 89–90, 91

Barton, Clara, 113
Better Angel, The (Morris), 114–115
Blake, William, 50
Bloom, Harold, 22
Boardman, Henry, 116
Brooks, David, 2
Brown, Lewy, 127, 128–129, 134

Cantor, Paul, 42
Chase, Salmon P., 49
Civil War, 110–113; George Whitman
    and, 112–113; Lincoln's leadership
    and humility and, 136–137. *See also*

hospitals, Whitman's volunteer
    work in
Clapp, Henry, 108–109
Clare, Ada, 109

death: democracy and immortality
    and, 101–103; great deeds and,
    100–101; reflections on in letter to
    Sawyer, 129; Whitman's hospital
    work and, 125, 134–135; Whitman's
    views on, 31, 93, 99–100
democracy: death, immortality,
    and contributions to, 101–103;
    Emerson's limited view of "masses"
    and, 5–7; feudalism as temptation
    in, 56–60; freedom of Soul and, 26;
    grass as Whitman's central image
    for, 26–27, 29–33, 47; heroes and
    heroism and, 69–70; inclusion
    and, 34–37; Whitman and spiritu-
    alization of, xi–xii, 2, 8, 24–25,
    40–41, 130–131, 133–137; Whitman
    sees dangers of democratic life,
    xii–xiii; Whitman's joy in indi-
    viduality as well as acceptance by
    others, 7–8. *See also* democratic
    heroism

democratic heroism: American examples of not kneeling and not compelling others to kneel, 73–78; Civil War soldiers and, 117, 118–119, 135; Whitman's creation of new language for, 118

Derrida, Jacques, 58

Dickinson, Emily, 5, 90

différance, Derrida and, 58

Dylan, Bob, 65

Emerson, Ralph Waldo: belief that society advances through great people, 41, 77, 135–136; heroes and culture, 77; influence on Whitman, 2–5; on *Leaves of Grass*, 9; poetry and struggle for originality, 2–5; request for American bard, 47; spiritual life and, 16; tension between individual and group and, 31–32; on Whitman, 133; Whitman's letters to, 107

Emerson, Ralph Waldo, works of: "American Scholar," 7; "Circles," 2, 4; "History," 4; "The Poet," 2–3, 4, 7; *Representative Men*, 77; "Self-Reliance," 2, 4, 6

empathy, 35–36

England, early American fascination with kings and nobles, 42

evil, Whitman's view of, 74–75

feudalism: Whitman's dislike of feudal literature, xii, 19, 25, 37, 42–43; Whitman's use of sun as image of, 53–60

Fletcher, Angus, 18

Folsom, Ed, 16

free verse, used in *Song of Myself*, 18

Freud, Sigmund, 57, 77

Frost, Robert, 50, 86

Frye, Northrop, 54

Fugitive Slave Law, 35

God: mentioned in letters to Sawyer, 128; Whitman on, 91–93; Whitman's hospital work and, 133–134

grass: sun as counterimage to, 58, 94; as Whitman's central image for democracy, 26–27, 29–33, 47

great deeds: death and, 100–101; Emerson and, 41, 77, 135–136; Whitman's questions about, 53–60; Whitman's questions about resolved in hospital work, 98, 135–138. *See also* democratic heroism

Greeley, Horace, 109

Gregg, Miss (hospital worker), 125–126

Group Psychology (Freud), 57

Hapgood, Lyman, 117–118

Haskell, Erastus, 124–125

Hegel, Friedrich, 82

heroism. *See* democratic heroism

Heyde, Charles L. (brother-in-law), 2

hierarchy, Whitman's dislike of, 41–43, 77

Homer, 17, 39, 72, 77

hospitals, Whitman's volunteer work in: as manifestation of poetic vision, 114, 119–121, 123–126, 134; nature of work, 112–116, 120, 121–126, 131; numbers of hospitals and conditions at, 115; paid work during time of, 117–118; soldiers as democratic heroes, 117, 118–119; Whitman's health and, 131–132, 133; Whitman's lodging at time of, 124

humility, greatness and, 135–138

Iliad (Homer), 17, 39
individuality, democracy and, 99
intermarriage, democracy and inclusion and, 34–35

James, William, 74
Jesus: as first real democrat, 81, 92; only figure from traditional religion respected by Whitman, 86; Whitman's dedivinizing and rebirth of humanity in America, 79–83; Whitman's reconfiguring of on behalf of democracy, 49–50, 67
Jones, John Paul, 76–78

Lawrence, D. H., 70
Leaves of Grass (Whitman): citizens and states and, 44–45; 1855 edition of, 15–16, 48–49, 105, 108; 1856 edition of, 107, 108; 1860 edition of, 107; 1892 deathbed edition of, 16, 33; Emerson on, 9; literary culture and time of writing of, xii, 19; Whitman's disappointment in reception of, 9. *See also* Whitman, Walt, works of
Lewis, R. W. B., 20
Lincoln, Abraham, 27, 35; dual nature of greatness and humility, 136–138; as embodiment of marriage of Self and Soul, 138; slavery and union, 110; Whitman's elegies for, 108, 137–138; Whitman sees in New York, 111

Marx, Karl, 67
marriage, mutually exclusive love and, 130
masturbation scene: Whitman's candor and self-exposure to reader, 64–65, 96, 98; Whitman's distress then understanding of, 61–64, 71
"Mending Wall" (Frost), 50
Menken, Adah, 109
Merrill, Christopher, 16
Milton, John, 17, 39, 41
Morris, Roy, Jr., 114–115

narcissism: kings and, 57; Whitman's celebration of body and, 52
nations, creative and human culture and, 26–27
New York Times, 116
New York Tribune, 112
nobility. *See* aristocracy

O'Connor, William and Nellie, 124

Paradise Lost (Milton), 17, 39, 41
Pfaff's, Whitman's Bohemian Brooklyn life and, 108–111
phrenology, Whitman and, 87
Plato, 26, 57, 77
Poirier, Richard, 87, 110
Pound, Ezra, 97
presence, democracy and, 99

rangers, Texas, massacre of, 73–75
Redpath, James, 122
religion: Americans and acceptance of, 91–93; compressed genealogy of religious practices, 89–90; Whitman and atheism, 89–90, 91; Whitman's choice of democracy over traditional religion, 84–87; Whitman's hospital work and, 134. *See also* God; Jesus
Representative Men (Emerson), 77
Republic (Plato), 57
Reynolds, David, 5, 110

Rivera, Diego, 68
Rorty, Richard, 37, 93, 97

Sawyer, Tom, 127–129, 134
Shakespeare, William, and Whitman's
  demystifying of nobility, 42–43, 54
Shelley, Percy Bysshe, 52
slavery: quadroon girl in catalogue of
  Americans, 40; Whitman's dislike
  of, 35, 110–111. *See also* Civil War
Song of Myself (Whitman), generally:
  as American quest of education
  and discovery, 8, 15–18, 23; autoerotic scene and, 61–65, 71, 96, 98;
  catalogue of individuals in American community, 38–40, 75, 137;
  edition of 1855, 83; engraving
  of Whitman and, 15, 16; as first
  significant use of free verse,
  18; gratitude, joy, and hymn to
  physical life, 51–52; identities and
  unity of states, 44–46; invitations,
  not edicts, of, 97; setting of standard
  for thoughts and actions, 138; tour
  of nation in, 69–70; Whitman's
  celebration in midpoint of, 48–49;
  Whitman's waiting for us at end of,
  xiii, 103, 138
Soul: differs from Christian Soul, 25;
  nakedness and vulnerability to new
  experiences, 20; physical marriage
  of Self and, 24–27, 28, 47; pride and
  sympathy and, 25–26; *Song of
  Myself* and inviting into world,
  17–18, 19–23; as unitary, 22
spiritual democracy, xi-xii, 2, 8, 24–25,
  40–41, 130–131; embodied in
  Whitman's hospital work, 133–137
stage drivers, Whitman's befriending
  of, 110, 113

state identities, and unity in U.S.,
  44–46, 47
Stevens, Wallace, 20, 71
sun: as counterimage to grass, 58, 94;
  as unity without diversity, 64–65;
  Whitman's use of as image of royal
  power and feudalism, 53–60
Symonds, John Addington, 64

"Tea at the Palaz of Hoon"
  (Stevens), 71
Thoreau, Henry David, 20
Twain, Mark, 59

unity, democracy and, 99

Varieties of Religious Experience
  (James), 74
Virgil, 17

Whitman, Andrew Jackson
  (brother), 1–2
Whitman, Edward (brother), 2
Whitman, George Washington
  (brother), 2, 112–113
Whitman, Hannah Louisa (sister), 2
Whitman, Jesse (brother), 1
Whitman, Louisa Van Velsor
  (mother), 1, 2; Whitman's letters to,
  117, 120–122, 126, 131–132
Whitman, Mary Elizabeth (sister), 2
Whitman, Nancy (sister-in-law), 1–2
Whitman, Thomas Jefferson
  (brother), 2, 115, 116
Whitman, Walt: appearance in 1860s,
  121–122; authority, identity, and
  relationship to readers, 94–98;
  Bohemian life in Brooklyn in
  1850s, 107–111; character of, xii,
  xiii, 9, 15; Civil War and, 110–113;